CW00815753

Praise for *Rise From The Dream*

"In *Rise From The Dream* Kostas Petrou shares his heart-breaking childhood and youth with raw and astute self-clarity. Repeatedly bullied, beaten and degraded from a very young age, Kostas unpacks his story with brutal honesty, never shying away or sugar coating the frightening and nasty realities. But ultimately the book offers up lessons in unfailing belief in self, in courage to make different choices, and in determination to reclaim a life pushed into a downward spiral.

"The book is a must read for all who have been bullied, disconnected, or devalued. It provides hope, insights and help in straight forward and relatable language. I wish I would have had access to it years ago. A definite recommend."

— Lori Dean, Radio Personality, Creator of Help!
My Mid-life Sucks! Radio show

"Kostas story is both very sad and uplifting at the same time. He is lucky to be alive and probably is only because he has a purpose that he needs to fulfill. It is wonderful to know that he is finally on his true path.

"His story about being bullied and a victim for much of

his life resonates with me as I have worked with many foster youth who have very similar stories to tell. It broke my heart to hear what he went through. He learned a valuable lesson when, in his own words, "My eyes caught sight of graffiti on one side of the wall that said, *'It does not matter what has happened in your life up until this point, what matters is, what you are going to do about it!'*

"The first question I asked each of my new clients upon our first meeting is, 'Do you plan to be a victim of your past and your experiences or do you want to take responsibility for your life and create a better future?' Each and everyone one of them said they wanted a better future. Some of them were able to create that better future, others were not as lucky as Kostas.

"Be strong when you read this book because as difficult as some of this is to read, remember that Kostas actually lived it and he survived it by never giving up on himself even when it would have been the easy thing to do. And to his credit, he turned those experiences around and is now in a position to be empathetic with and have compassion for others who have low self-esteem and lack confidence."

— Julia Neiman,
The Youth Entrepreneurship Coach

"Life is full of struggles and obstacles, and Kostas Petrou knows all about this. He is one of the strong ones who dared to pick himself up each time he fell (or is pushed) and dared to struggle to realise his dreams. His messages should be shared and will help to give strength to anyone who is living through tough times."

— Alexandra Panayotou Motivational Speaker,
Writer, Ultra Endurance Runner

RISE
FROM
THE DREAM

*A Candid Account Of One Man's Rise
From Bullying And Homelessness
To The Stage – How He Reset His
Thinking And Created His Path*

KOSTAS PETROU
With
CHERRY-ANN CAREW

Rise From The Dream

A Candid Account Of One Man's Rise From Bullying And Homelessness To The Stage – How He Reset His Thinking And Created His Path

This book is dedicated to my wife to be, Elisavet. You are the greatest gift life has blessed me with, and I thank God for you daily. I love you angel of mine.

TABLE OF CONTENTS

ACKNOWLEDGEMENTS

S PECIAL THANKS TO God. Without him nothing is
possible.

Cherry Ann Carew, thank you for agreeing to
collaborate with me on this book. You believed in me and
my story, a story that I hope will enhance the lives of those
who read it.

Mum, Dad, George, Helen and Anna. Words cannot
express how much you mean to me and thank you hardly
seems enough. I love you guys.

Midera and Badera, you welcomed me with open arms
into your family and treat me like a son. For that I thank you.

Tony, a true friend. You are always in my heart. R.I.P.

Respect to Frank Bruno, one of the nicest people I've
had the privilege of meeting. Your words filled me with
inspiration and I appreciate you supporting this book.

Sincere appreciation to all of you who endorsed this
book, I am deeply honoured.

Thank you to everyone who supported me in my football,
boxing and career journey. And a special thanks to those of
you who told me I would never become successful in life,
you were my motivation during the toughest of times.

To you, dear reader, 'Don't just go through it, grow
through it!'

AUTHOR'S NOTE

THIS BOOK IS a work of nonfiction. I have rendered the events thoughtfully and truthfully as I have recalled them. Some names and descriptions of individuals and places have been changed and, or, deliberately referred to vaguely in order to respect their privacy. While circumstances and conversations portrayed within come from my avid recollection of them, they are not meant to represent precise timelines of events or exact word-for-word replication of my experience. They are told in a way that evokes the real feeling and meaning of what was said and my view of what happened to me, in keeping with the true essence of the mood and spirit of those moments that shaped my life.

WHY I WROTE THIS BOOK

HAVE YOU EVER felt like you wanted to quit? Maybe you feel a bit lost in your career or personal life. Maybe you feel like you are at rock bottom and you don't have the strength to get back up. Then again, maybe you are doing well in life, but something... something is missing.

Whichever it is, this book will take you on a journey that will inspire you to stay strong when you feel weak, to make you think like a champion when you want to quit. It will help you to find the correct path when you are feeling lost and give you life lessons that will enable you to go forward to be the best you can be.

How can this book do that? Because I have overcome all of the above and then some and I share my trials, from being bullied to being homeless, to my triumphs – becoming the number one top-earner as a recruitment consultant and following my life purpose, that is, as a motivational coach and speaker.

But this book is not only about my experiences, it's function is to demonstrate that no matter how impossible things may seem, no matter how low you may feel, no matter how people bring you down, or try to bring you down, you can achieve absolutely anything if you develop the mind-set that you have what it takes to go after your dreams.

The aim of this book is to motivate and inspire you. It dares you to dream and then take action to turn that dream into your reality like I did!

INTRODUCTION

B ULLYING HAS BEEN a problem among young kids and teens from time immemorial. Interestingly, it started as a way to break the ice between peers to make a newcomer feel welcomed, in a fun way, in a new setting. Over time, however, it turned into a form of harassment.

Unfortunately, many children experience it in some shape or form, whether it's verbal — name-calling to cause emotional pain, psychological — being excluded, or dealing with malicious rumors, or physical bullying with the conscious intent to hurt — hitting, pushing, or taking one's possessions.

Naturally, this crosses all boundaries of fun and goes beyond the normal tolerance limit of any human being. Bullying is hurtful and demeaning.

Sadly, this behaviour happens in many environments, most often inside schools and the playground. This was the case for Kostas Petrou. This was where his nightmare started.

When Kostas first connected with me, he said that people who knew about his experience of being bullied and being homeless voiced their opinions that he should share his background, and he'd decided to do so in book form; I wanted to hear his story.

To say it deeply affected me would be putting it mildly. Maybe it's because I'm a mother and I can't fathom the thought of one of my children being bullied. Perhaps it's because I've never been close enough to anyone who has been victimized through bullying, or been aware. Sure, I've watched the news, movies and read about sad instances that led children to take drastic measures to gain some peace of mind, but I was still perturbed.

Worse, what was even more shocking, was hearing that it wasn't only other kids who bullied him, but teachers, too! Maybe I am naïve, but I can't get my head around that one.

Still, as is expected, when one loses his self-confidence and self-esteem, he falls into *learned helplessness*. Kostas was one such victim and it affected him in many areas including poor educational performance, feeling disconnected from his peers and, as a result, he was unable to make friends. He was filled with frustration and resentment, which led to him giving up his dream of becoming a professional footballer.

In addition, he not only felt vulnerable, but demoralised and subsequently demotivated, further leading him to make choices that changed the direction of his life at a young age.

The good news is Kostas got his life back on an even keel and now works with people to help them overcome their stumbling blocks to go and live their dream. I was sold by his selfless act and, thus, 'Rise From the Dream' was born.

This book is but a stepping stone for Kostas as he continues to move forward, demonstrating that you can rise above it all and I feel privileged to be a part of his success story.

To your success

Cherry-Ann Carew
Award Finalist and Multi-bestselling Author
Founder of Writetastic Solutions
California

Chapter 1

THE JOYS OF INNOCENCE

'In their innocence, very young children know them-selves to be light and love. If we will allow them, they can teach us to see ourselves the same way.'
— Michael Jackson

M Y OLDER BROTHER, George, absolutely loved football and wanting to be just like him, I grew to love the 'Beautiful Game,' too. I called George the brain because he was very intelligent and in my young eyes, was a walking encyclopedia, especially when it came to football. Every weekend, he flipped to the sports tables section of The Sports Argus , our local newspaper, and memorize the football results for every game that took place in the Premier League and Division One, that particular weekend. Afterward, he put the paper down and tested himself; hence my nickname for him, the brain.

One time, George kicked the make-believe football, a cushion, and I dived to save it, pretending to be England's second-most capped goalkeeper, David Seaman, at the peak of his career as Arsenal and England goalkeeper. George allowed me to concede a goal so he could run to the window and pretend to celebrate in front of 40,000 fans by making a loud cheering noise whilst jumping in the air.

I have pleasant memories of us battering that cushion, along with unpleasant ones, as well. On one occasion, it smashed an ornament and on another, I kicked it with such force, it knocked the food my mum was carrying right out of her hands as she walked toward the dining room.

Of course, I ran… around and around the dining table as she chased me whilst telling me off. This then became fun for me and I giggled; she grew angrier. In time, though, seeing the comical side of things, she softened and laughed her head off then hugged and kissed me, calling me her baby. I was eight or nine, and had no interest in any other sport; playing football was my passion and my favourite daily pastime.

My sisters, Helen and Anna, were busy doing their own things. Helen was obsessed with becoming a singer and spent most of her time singing. Anna, on the other hand, spent every available second with her friends.

I felt blessed having a close-knit family. We went to restaurants together and shared once-a-year holidays, such as trips to other European countries like, Cyprus, Italy, and Spain.

For the most part, we all got along well with one another. Of course, there were the usual sibling scraps, and my father, who was hot-headed, would flip at the drop of a coin if he found out someone was disrespecting him in one way or another.

His hot-headedness may have had something to do with him being a British boxing champion during the 1980s. His bad temper generated a lot of fear in all of us. Yet, when he wasn't riled up, he was an amazing dad. When we played, he called me 'Little Tank,' in reference to his nickname in the boxing world, which was 'The Greek Tank.'

Dad and I had a fantastic relationship. He was a strong male figure for me and very much a family man.

In contrast, my mum was bubbly and outgoing. She is one of those individuals who would have a conversation with anyone and everybody who would listen. And she has a presence about her. When she walked into a room, all eyes seem to land on her.

While Dad was stoic, yet approachable, Mum and I would sit and chat and cuddle on the settee. She might allow me to sneak a chocolate in without letting Dad know. If he found out, he'd moan, because he did not want us children to load up on junk food, which was reserved for weekends.

Overall, our household was generally lively and safe when you take into consideration that we lived in West Midlands, Birmingham, to be exact, which is pretty much a concrete jungle, being an industrialized area.

Still, I went through the normal school system. However, while in primary school, I was mixing with naughty children and my mum was concerned that I was being influenced and not in a good way.

I grew boisterous and did silly things like doing a number two in the bushes! This, along with other antics, didn't bode well with her, and the last straw was when I got suspended from school after play fighting with another kid and broke his nose. I was, as expected, suspended. I was more upset that I hurt my friend than about being suspended, as I had no idea what the implications were of not being allowed to attend school temporarily.

My mother did, and promptly decided to transfer me to another school. She was of the opinion that if I didn't get away from such bad influence, my innocence would be knocked out of me and I would end up being a little terror.

It was not an easy process. Mum had to jump through hoops, because the school governing board did not want to have me transferred. After a lot of persistence and tears from my mother's end, I was subsequently transferred to a highly reputable school.

The problem was I was so busy being naughty in my other school I hadn't learn much, so when I was thrown in amongst well-educated, well-schooled clever children, I stood out like a sore thumb, to coin an overused cliché.

In addition, I was geeky looking and wore huge glasses; my physique was small for my age and I was the least well-spoken student in the entire school.

I was not to know what a cut-throat institution I'd entered.

Chapter 2

RUDE AWAKENING

'I used to love school until everybody got old enough to point and laugh.'
— *A. S. King*

A S I ENTERED this new world of academia, I took my innocent way of thinking with me, which was, the world is a beautiful place and everyone is loving and caring like my family. My innocence was knocked out of me not long after starting when my teacher asked, 'What's an elephant's nose called, Kostas?'

I was stuck. I didn't know. 'Erm—'

'C'mon, Kostas!'

I didn't answer and she proceeded to instruct the students to write the answer on a piece of paper.

After collecting mine and glancing at it, she erupted with laughter. I had never seen anybody laugh so hard before. When she could find her voice, she told me to stand before the class and said, 'Kostas, tell the class what you wrote down as your answer.'

'Erm… A cumon, Miss,' I said and felt my face heat up.

She burst into laughter again and so did the entire class. Not only that, but they pointed at me. Embarrassment filled my body and I wanted the ground to swallow me up.

But the teacher wasn't finished with me yet. She interrupted every class that was in session and made me stand up in front of them to repeat my answer. As a result, everyone laughed at me, including the head teacher!

From that point onwards, whenever the head teacher saw me, he waved a hand in my face and in a patronizing voice greeted me with, 'Hellooo Kostaaas, duuurrr, todaaay isss Mooonday.' This was usually in front of other kids and shouts of, 'Dumb ass,' followed.

It was a rude awakening. I did not see any of that coming. Not from the teachers, and certainly not being placed in front of the entire school to be mocked and laughed at, because I wasn't as clever as the other students. In addition, my nerd-like appearance was comical to them.

I not only felt demoralised, but I was filled with confusion; I did not quite understand if this sort of behaviour was normal school etiquette, since I had not experienced any form of abuse in my other primary school; in fact, up until then, I had never experienced any abuse, and couldn't understand why everyone was being horrible to me. I wanted to fit in.

'How come when the head teacher sees me in class he waves his hand in my face and says, 'Hellooo Kostaaas, duuurrr, todaaay isss Mooonday,'' I asked my dad.

'Show me exactly what he does,' he said.

I imitated the teacher and he went ballistic.

'Cheeky bastard! How dare he belittle my son like that? Who does he think he is?'

He wound himself up thinking about it until he found his way to the school, where he had a heated conversation with the head teacher about belittling me. Thankfully, he didn't do anything he would later regret. He visited the school twice thereafter, but I was concerned that he would hurt someone and never again told him about any other incidents.

Nevertheless, I decided I would be extra nice to everyone and was excessively polite to both teachers and students. I even held the door open for them. It made no difference. I became the target for my teacher, especially, to put me down in the presence of fellow students, who sniggered when she made snide remarks, which seemed to give her pleasure. She would deliberately ask me questions so that she could mock me.

By condoning the students' sniggering, naturally they felt they had carte blanche to add to it, and add to it they did. I became their object for mockery, whereby they would mimic the teacher when she ridiculed me and it extended into assembly and into the playground.

In no time, the mimicry turned to verbal bullying and name calling. You see, I'm mixed race — Greek and English. I was different. I didn't fit in with the English kids because I didn't look Caucasian and my name is Greek, which was fodder for their name calling, that ranged from 'cost of coffee,' 'cost of petrol,' 'lost ass,' to name a few.

In addition, I did not fit into the Greek community, because you were not seen as truly Greek if you did not speak the language, I did not. Also, if one's parents were not a part of the community - my parents were not, that added to the exclusion. Essentially, I was not accepted from either side of the fence.

Yet, I continued to work hard at making friends, but it was no use. The situation grew worse, because the teachers and students saw that I really wanted to be their friend and read my desperate attempts to fit in as weakness, which they exploited.

I got an early lesson that people are not as nice as I thought they were. That there was nastiness in people; that they don't care how much they hurt you; that they will, no matter how much you try, how much you plead, how much you reason with them, continue to be cruel.

I had always looked for the good in people, but as time went on there seemed to be none in those I was surrounded by, excluding my family. I started to see the world as a very dark and lonely place as the verbal abuse became a daily constant in my young life and I didn't know how to deal with it.

I felt as if I was swimming against the tide, and so like a tortoise, I crawled into my shell filled with rejection; I locked myself away in loneliness.

I became a loner.

Chapter 3

THE LONG AND HELLISH ROAD

'Pulease, pulease leave me alone... For Christ's sake leave me alone'.
— *Vladimir Nabokov*

IT WAS A long, frustrating and emotionally draining few years, but I made it through primary school and headed into secondary school.

It was quite a strange feeling listening to the teacher as she called out the names of the schools each student would attend. Many groups of children were thrilled that they would be together and voiced it by saying, 'Yeah, we're going to be together.'

I didn't have anyone to share that moment with. I was the only kid from my class attending a different secondary school. I was; however, glad to move on because my brother and one of my sisters were students there.

Rumour had it though, that the school was rough; what that meant, I wasn't entirely sure. Also, someone mentioned that going there would change my life. I had no choice in the matter anyway and thought further that I can make a new start, which included going to the gym and getting my body strong. I was going to transform myself into somebody else, because I was frustrated with how I was treated and fed up with being bullied. I was going into my new school as a new person.

My self-talk was just that. Talk. I lost interest before I even started working out, but sometimes took a trip to the gym to pass the time. Of course, there were no changes to my body.

Nevertheless, my lack of physicality didn't hinder me and my first year in secondary school turned out to be enjoyable.

During the first school assembly, all the students were introduced so we got to meet the children we were going to spend the next five years with. Before I knew it, I was making friends and I thought, *'this isn't so bad.'* And it wasn't. I did quite well that year academic wise and really enjoyed it.

For the first time in years, I walked around school free of derogatory remarks coming at me from all directions. Perhaps it was because my sister and brother, who were pretty popular, attended, though my brother was in his final year.

During my second year, I was placed into different classes and groups. Things continued as in the previous year until one summer's day, after enjoying a game of football as part of physical education (PE), a friend came up to me and whispered, 'Kostas, those two boys over there are planning to beat you up.'

I looked at him and laughed. 'That's silly. What are you talking about? Why do they want to beat me up? What have I done to them?'

I was used to being verbally abused in primary school; but I had never been beaten up so I didn't quite know why those boys wanted to hurt me.

I discreetly looked over to where they stood. They were whispering amongst themselves. I recognize them from the same school year as me and knew their names, though they weren't my friends.

'I'm going to talk to them,' I told my friend.

I walked up to them and said, 'Hi, guys, do you want some money for lunch? I've got £5.00.' I reached into my pocket and pulled out a £5.00 note. 'Take it.'

They looked at me and started laughing.

'I don't mind,' I told them, 'I can get more money from my sister.'

They put their arms around me and said, 'You're alright, you're okay.'

I was relieved and thought, yes, I made friends. It's okay now. It's finished with.

'I'm glad that you're happy. Go and spend it on whatever you want. Have some nice lunch,' I added before walking towards the bottom of the field. The pitch was based at the top, quite a distance away from the school building.

My instincts, however, told me to get away from them quickly. If they jumped me, the teachers wouldn't see, as they were on the far side of the pitch, about half a mile away. The boys were bigger than me and even if I attempted to defend myself, I just wouldn't be able to.

I quickened my steps, but before I could get into stride, I felt a blow on my back that sent me flat on the ground and then punches were raining all over my back and the back of my head.

The boys dragged me down the hill and continued pounding into me. I was never punched in my face, so I stiffened and hugged my body as tears flooded my eyes and

I shouted at them, 'Why are you doing this? What have I done to you? Please leave me alone!'

'You little Greek bastard. You little Greek bastard,' they ranted as they continued to punch me.

Eventually they stopped and ran off laughing. I reached for my bag, clung to it and stayed still for a while then crawled over to a corner where no one could see me. I sat there for about forty-minutes crying my eyes out, because I knew then that my remaining school years weren't going to be a good journey at all. It was going to be a very bad time. I wore a gold cross underneath my T-shirt that was given to me when I was baptised and I reached for it and prayed to God for help.

After crying and praying for this incident to be a one off, I made myself get up, but my body ached. There were still people on the field, though they couldn't see me. I was embarrassed beyond words that I had been beaten up. My father, whom I was immensely proud of, was a former boxing champion and I was his 'Little Tank.' I always had it in my head that no one would physically touch me due to my dad's reputation. It just didn't make sense.

I waited until most of the students returned to their classes and made my way through a path where there were the least people. It was difficult walking straight. My body hurt.

I walked into the art class and immediately spotted two friends of the bullies sitting at the back. This is going to get worse. I continued to the front and sat in the first row. I felt a level of protection being close to my teacher, though only temporarily. About twenty minutes into the class, a student handed me a note that read: You Illegal immigrant you're gonna get fucked up.

My heart pounded uncontrollably after reading the note and a sinking, lonely feeling washed over me. Then the realisation that I was trapped and had absolutely no one to turn to for help paralyzed me to the point that I was scared to walk into my next class in case they caught me.

Once again, I became a target for bullying. This time it was worse, because it wasn't just verbal—it was physical. I was spat on, called a Greek bastard, a Greek Paki, an illegal immigrant, told to go back to my country, every racist and crude slur imaginable, I was called.

The teachers were worse than the primary school teachers. They knew I was being bullied, yet did nothing about it. They looked the other way. In fact, they added to it.

On one occasion, all the students were lined up in the school indoor football area. A teacher pointed to me and said, 'Cock ass, I mean, Kostas, come here.'

The whole class collapsed in laughter. I stepped forward, my face bright red from humiliation and my head down. I couldn't bear to look up knowing everyone was looking at me.

'What do you want to be when you're older?' he asked.

Along with being grossly embarrassed, my mind was racing as to what I should say so I didn't cause further embarrassment. I wanted to be a footballer so bad and I thought maybe if I told him my dream, he'd give me an opportunity to play for the district, which was a big deal.

'I want to be a footballer,' I told him.

'Who's your idol?'

'My dad.'

The whole class started laughing again.

'You're a joke. Go back in your line,' he dismissed me.

And so with my head down, I rejoined the line until next time. There was no respite. It was constant. No matter what avenue I took, some form of verbal abuse was thrown my way.

As time went on, the bullies formed a gang and got into all sorts of criminal activities. It wasn't uncommon to see the police coming to the school about their involvement in a stabbing or another criminal act. They were arrested, but would always be released with warnings because they were underage.

On occasion, one of the bullies would do something good in class and since I desperately wanted to be liked, I would say, 'Well done. I could never have done that.'

My observations and comments meant nothing to them. All they cared about was humiliating and hurting me. I never understood why they hated me.

I didn't feel sorry for myself. I wanted to get past this stage, to get over it, to forever get away from this abuse. Neither did I tell my parents. After seeing how my dad reacted when I was in primary school, I was afraid that he would hurt someone and I didn't want him to get into any trouble. However, he came close to finding out one time when I faked being sick so I didn't have to go to school.

It so happened that one of my younger, loud mouth cousins, who attended the same school had, unbeknownst to me, seen a guy punch me in the stomach as I walked across the link bridge to the school.

I didn't see her; neither did I see the punch coming. I buckled to the ground, I was so winded. I could hardly breathe. It was one of the worst pains I had experienced up to that moment.

I don't know how I managed, but I snuck into an empty staff room and sat in unbearable pain for how long I couldn't tell. I was positive I was going to die.

The following day, I laid on the settee faking feeling sick so I wouldn't have to go to school. My loudmouth cousin stopped by and I answered the door. After the usual pleasantries, she asked if I was going to school. I told her no, and she said, 'Stop being a weakling, come on, come to school and face it.'

'Shut up and go away,' I snapped at her. I wanted her to go

away quickly; I didn't want anyone to hear our conversation and question what was going on.

'Come on,' she persisted.

'Get lost and leave me alone,' I said through gritted teeth, pushed her through the door, closed it and walked straight into Dad.

I knew I was in trouble when I saw his facial expression. It didn't take much to ascertain what mood he was in. One look at his face told you, and at that moment he looked like a monster. He grabbed hold of my jumper, pulled me towards him and asked, 'What was that about?'

'I'm really not well. I just want to be left alone,' I replied and felt my eyes welling up.

He pulled me even closer and said, 'If anyone's bullying you, I want you to go in there and I want you to rip their heads off.'

This was so typical of Dad; lash out with words in temper and when he cooled down, acknowledged what he said was wrong and see reason. Still, his words did not do much to help me, because I didn't have any confidence.

'I wouldn't let nobody bully me,' I said like I was Mr. tough guy. 'I ain't letting nobody bully me. I want to be left alone.' I disengaged myself from his hold and walked off.

His reaction sealed the deal for me. I was never, ever going to tell him I was being bullied at school. He would go crazy, absolutely crazy.

Interestingly, the bullies made fun of a few other children, but not to the extent that they tormented me. It seemed that because I was of Greek heritage, I was different in their eyes and the fact that my dad was a former British boxing champion somehow pissed them off even more. Often, when they were beating me up, they would say, 'Your dad's a big, tough boxer, eh! Your dad's a faggot, or your dads a brain damaged bum!'

Now, my dad was everything to me, my life, my hero, so to hear them verbally abusing him affected me more than the actual pain they inflicted on me. I really idolised my father. Once, whilst he was boxing a former world title contender and well-known commentator said, 'Kostas Petrou breaks his opponent's hearts because he doesn't take a backward step. The other guy gives it everything he can and next thing you know, he comes storming back at you. He does this so often.'

During his boxing heyday, my dad carried himself with such presence that when he walked the streets, people turned to look at him. I observed this on many occasions, such as events and when we went out for a meal. People vied for his attention and wanted to become acquainted with him. They often stared, pointed at him and said, 'That's Kostas Petrou.'

I understood why. He had an amazing physique, was strong, with character and a commanding presence along with it.

Dad had the same attitude out of the ring, too. He wouldn't back down from anyone and I used to think, 'Wow! I want to be like him one day. I want people to respect me like that.' Perhaps it was because I was quite shy that I related to him. Though he was perceived as fearless, he was actually pretty shy, too.

As the bullying continued, I became more withdrawn, while my love for the sport of football increased and it became my outlet. I decided then that I wanted to be a professional footballer and that burning desire was ignited within me. I also became obsessed with watching Manchester's United David Beckham play. I watched his free kicks, his corners, his set pieces over and over and over again. I wanted to perfect his technique.

I was not naturally gifted in the game, but I knew how

to play, along with the rules and was prepared to work hard no matter how much pain the bullies put me through. They were not going to stop me from training and following my dream of becoming a pro footballer.

So I took my football to the top of the field and would practice on my own for hours and hours until I became pretty skilled. I always ensured that I kicked the ball towards the goal post, for the reason that behind it were bushes and beyond, a gate with big gap. It was my quick getaway exit should I need to run away from the bullies. Sometimes they'd spot me before I saw them and would beat me up. Sometimes I managed to get my ball and run away before they could get me. At other times, I wasn't able to get my ball before running away, but I was never deterred from playing my beloved football.

I later joined a local football team and played well. I scored goals and was 'Man of the Match' on numerous occasions. After each game I went home. I did not mix with anyone. The reason was, outside of my family, I didn't know how to socialize with other people. I'd never learned that skill. The only thing I knew was expecting violence. I didn't know how to behave around children, specially.

My feeling was that everybody was out to get me and I was on constant alert, waiting to be verbally attacked, or physically assaulted. I didn't talk to anyone unless it was necessary to the game, in case I got laughed at or bullied so I kept quiet and kept my distance.

There were times when I didn't want to go to matches, not because I didn't want to play, but I was so socially awkward, it was uncomfortable. Dad always urged me to, 'Get stuck in and talk to the lads and be a part of the team.'

I tried so hard to make him proud because he was certain that my career was in football and so did I.

Chapter 4

OPPORTUNITY KNOCKS

'Everything negative - pressure, challenges - is all an opportunity for me to rise.'

— *Kobe Bryant*

Though I played for the local football club, I wanted to continue to really work on my skills. The problem was it was difficult practicing on the school grounds. I couldn't focus, as I constantly looked over my shoulder to avoid getting jumped and beaten up.

During a walk one afternoon after school – I liked taking long walks on my own to reflect and think—I aimlessly headed in a direction I never had before and ended up on what seemed to be a country lane.

About two miles in, I couldn't believe my eyes when I arrived at the back of Birmingham City Football Club training ground. I increased my pace toward the gate that was identical to the one at my school. It was, of course, locked. Could there be a way in like at my school? I wondered.

I inspected one side. It was solid. Moving over to the other end, lo and behold, there was a gap that I could tell was deliberately forced open and wide enough for me to climb through. I couldn't believe my luck, so I did!

The pitch was beautifully laid out, I was in awe that my feet were actually on it and when I got closer to the goal, I became excited and started kicking the ball, imagining that I was at Wembley Stadium.

Being completely on my own without having to look over my shoulders playing a game that brought me peace was… well, I was in seventh heaven.

When I calmed down, I looked around and saw another gate about a hundred yards away that led to the first team players training area. I was tempted to walk through, but refrained. I didn't want to push my luck. I was pleased as punch about my new finding, it became my secret hide-out and I snuck in to practice every afternoon in peace and quiet for maybe a month, until one afternoon when I heard someone shouting at me.

I turned and saw a man dressed in the Birmingham City Football Club kit walking towards me. My first thought was to run before he called the police and I'd be arrested and charged for trespassing on private property.

Instead, I froze as wild thoughts flew through my mind… he was going to kick me off the pitch. I have to find somewhere else to play. Here, I found peace and quiet to play my football. I felt gutted at that thought. My sanctuary was exposed. I was desperate to stay training on this pitch because the surface was amazing, unlike the muddy, grassless patch of land that served as a pitch at school. Not to mention the wonderful goalposts with nets! Playing on that pitch made me feel… like a professional footballer.

'What are you doing on the pitch?' the man asked, as he drew closer to me.

I noticed a combination of anger and 'I feel sorry for you, kid', look on his face.

My heart was racing faster than I had ever remembered. 'I've got nowhere else to play, can I just stay here? I won't do any harm to anybody', I said in one breath.

'Well, if you're going to play, come and play with us', he said.

I was expecting him to read me the riot act, not offer an invitation to play with the other players.

It took me a few moments to compute that he actually did invite me to join the youth team training session. Once I did, words cannot explain the joy that flooded through my body. I was shocked and elated at the same time, because my life revolved around making it as a pro footballer. The joy was replaced with nerves and I suddenly felt cold and shaky.

'…but this is Birmingham City Football Club', I stated the obvious. 'I've been contacting you.' It was true. At intervals, I used to call the club and ask for talent scouts to come and watch me play at the local club; nothing ever came of it. 'Are you actually asking me to come and have a trial with you? Can I have trials with you there?'

'Ah…kind of a trial. Come and play with us. If you're going to play on the club's pitch, you might as well play with us today, but you can't come back again.'

I think he felt sorry for me because I was a kid on my own.

'Are you from around here?' he asked as we walked.

'Yes.'

'What's your name?'

I was worried about being discriminated against, so I told him, 'Kos.'

He gave me a curious look, nodded and said, 'I'm Dean.'

When we reached where the others players were, he told

them, 'Kos is joining us for a session today.' Turning to me, he asked, 'What position do you play?'

'Midfield.'

'Okay, join the team in bibs and let's get going.'

I played hard and must have looked like an absolute lunatic charging forward, slide tackling and basically giving my all. I had never run around a pitch nonstop and worked so hard in my life. I did not stop until the game was over.

Afterwards, the lads walked into the changing room, followed by the coaches and I was left on my own. Dean didn't say anything to me. In tears, I stormed off. I was sobbing from frustration because I felt I had an opportunity and nothing was going to come from it.

As I walked through the carpark that housed the player's fancy sports cars, and which led to the main gate, I saw Robbie Savage, a popular footballer and probably the best-known player for the club at the time, standing next to his Lamborghini. Before I could take in the fact that I was up close to such an extravagant and amazing vehicle and seeing a famous footballer player, I heard Dean shout my name.

I turned around and sprinted towards him. Tears streamed down my face and I wiped them away as I ran, though my eyes were still watery. I didn't want him to see that I was crying. I wanted to be a macho man.

'What's the matter with you?' he asked when I reached him.

'Nothing, I'm just happy that I had the opportunity to play.' My eyes started filling up again. I couldn't control the tears.

'I want you to come back tomorrow.'

'Wow! That's amazing,' I said. 'I can't wait to tell my dad, he always thought I would have a career in sport like he did.'

'Who's your dad?'

'Kostas Petrou.'

'The boxer?'

'Yes,' I said, excited that he knew of my dad.

'I know who your dad is. I used to watch him all the time.'

That was sort of my ticket in, an out-of-the-blue trial.

'Anyway, I want you to join the youth team.'

I was speechless for a few seconds. 'Are you being serious? This is a dream come true for me,' I stuttered. 'Thank you so much, thank you.' My eyes got watery again, but I pulled myself together.

I went for secondary trials after our first meeting, but at that point I knew that I was going to be accepted, because Dean, who ran the youth team for whatever reason had taken to me and was already having conversations with my mum on the phone.

When I started as an official youth team member, I felt as if my life had taken a turn for the better. I realised that hard work and non-stop dedication really does get results and mine was playing for a professional football club that was in the premier league. It didn't matter that I was in the academy.

Chapter 5

BEATEN DOWN

'Being defeated is often a temporary condition. Giving up is what makes it permanent.'
— *Marilyn vos Savant*

IT WAS TOWARDS the end of my secondary schooling when I joined the youth team and everyone was talking about what their plans were after they left school; who would be attending college, take vocational courses, those sorts of things.

I happened to be in the changing room, well, hiding, really, after playing football in PE. I usually left five minutes earlier so that I could change and be out of there before the other students went in. However, on this occasion I didn't make it out in time. When I heard them coming, I slipped into the shower cubicle and pulled the curtain, hoping that no one would want to take a shower before leaving.

They breezed in, chatting away and I heard a few of the guys saying they've got trials at Birmingham City Football

Club. I was stunned. I just couldn't seem to get away from them. I sunk my head and hoped that they wouldn't make it into the Youth Team. If they did, they would ruin everything for me.

Distraught hearing this news, I began to pray. I prayed for them, too, which was difficult for me to do, but I remembered what I was taught from the Bible about turning the other cheek.

In the midst of my prayers, the shower curtain slid open. After the guy registered his surprise at seeing me sitting on the floor, he kicked me straight in the face. My head flew back and smashed into the tap that was directly behind my head. I was convinced that my skull was cracked open.

The sound of my head hitting the tap was so loud everyone in the changing room went silent for a few seconds. It also shocked the kicker, but when the others started laughing, he kicked me a few more times and they all walked out.

As was expected, an enormous lump grew at the back of my head. I never knew a lump could swell so big on anyone's head, not to mention the continuous throb. As always, I covered up my wounds. I bought the biggest adjustable cap I could find.

I was walking through the lounge at home a few days later when my mum came up to me and said jokingly, 'Why are you wearing that silly hat all the time? Take it off.' She reached over to lift it off from the back and I yelled, 'Aww!' The lump was still tender.

'What's wrong with you?' she asked surprised at my reaction.

'Nothing. Your nail caught the back of my head,' I quickly retorted.

'Stop messing about and stop being a weakling. I hardly touched you.'

'Yeah, yeah,' I said playfully, adjusted the cap and walked out the room.

It took nearly two weeks for the swelling to go down.

***

I found out that two of the bullies were successful with their trials and would join the academy. As if that wasn't bad enough, I was disheartened when we were all introduced to each other to see two others were accepted. They eyeballed me with point blank cold eyes that said, 'You ain't getting away from us. We're going to make your head a football.'

They started to really get inside my head and dominate my thoughts and I became more of a loner and didn't mix with anyone, unless we were on the pitch.

My journey home required that I walk past a bus stop. It became common for them to wait for me there, where they pulled me in and beat the crap out of me, along with the usual verbal abuse.

During a beating one time, one of the bullies said, 'We're getting older. Now it's your family's time. Your sister's hot.'

On another occasion, the same bully went into detail about what he was going to do to her and added that he'd, 'Make her their Ho!'

I was, naturally, protective of my sisters and my family as a whole. When they said derogatory things about my sisters, I developed a rage like none I had experienced before.

Still, when I wasn't being bullied, I focused on football. It was the only thing that made me happy. Playing football allowed me to forget about being bullied and I was able to express myself.

To add to my thrill of being in the football world, ex-professional footballer and European Champion for Aston Villa, Dennis Mortimer was added to Dean's team of coaches. I was ecstatic to be trained by him and spent a lot of time talking to him, which pissed off the bullies. They saw me as the kid that hung around the coach doing his head in by asking him a lot of questions.

At times we went on away trips and I couldn't get enough of it. We were on an away trip near London one day and before the team started warming up, I kicked the ball way over the fence; nothing unusual about that, one of the ball boys, or someone else usually went to fetch it. We played the game and after the match one of the bullies' friend, John, came up to me and said, 'Kostas, you fucking dickhead, you kicked my ball over the fence.'

I had completely forgotten about that, but to avoid an altercation, I told him, 'It's alright; I'll go and get it. I thought somebody would have gotten it by now, but it's cool. I'll get it.'

'It's too late now. I'm going to get it myself, but you're a dickhead.'

My breathing stopped. The pressure and torment I had endured through the years was taking its toll on me. I dropped my head and walked towards the changing rooms. Why couldn't they be normal with me like they were with the other lads? Was it so much to ask? I couldn't catch a break.

A few minutes later, he joined me in the changing rooms.

'Oi, you ignorant little twat!'

'What's the problem now? What's the problem,' I repeated nervously.

'I'm your problem. Wait until you get outside.'

'Why? What have I done to you? You got your ball back?'

Exasperated, I said, 'John, I'll buy you another ball,' which had no relevance, because he had his ball in his hand. He just wanted to pick on me.

'I don't want you to buy me another ball. Don't think you can just buy things to get yourself out of trouble.'

His comment made me realise that the bullies told him about me, because they used to tell me in school that I was always trying to pay them to be friends with me. I ignored him, zipped my bag up and went to sit on the coach that left not long after to take us home.

Though I enjoyed playing with other teams, I did not enjoy the trips whatsoever. There was no camaraderie, though I longed for and really wanted it.

About an hour and a half into the journey, the driver brought the coach to a stop at a service station. As always, everyone got out to stretch their legs, use the loo and, or, get some food.

I lagged behind while some of the players walked off; I wanted to stay close to the football coaches to avoid being jumped by the bullies. They were going to grab a bite at Burger King. The problem was some of the players also hung around them. I couldn't have it both ways, so I followed them.

After eating, everyone made their way back to the coach. As I headed in the same direction, three guys came out from behind the bushes and grabbed me by my chest, threw me up against the wall and started punching me in my stomach.

Something clicked inside me, and the realisation that I did not need to put up with the abuse anymore bolted through me. School was over. Playing football was a choice. 'I'm not taking this anymore. I don't need to go through this. Anything's better than this. That's it. No more. I'm not coming back.'

My spirit was broken and in that instant I decided to walk away from the game I loved most in the world. I would be lost without my football, but it was clear that leaving the team was the only way for me to maintain normalcy in my life.

Chapter 6

TWO BROKEN HEARTS

'Sometimes, in order to follow our moral compass and, or, our hearts, we have to make unpopular decisions or stand up for what we believe in.'
— *Tabatha Coffey*

COULD I GO through with it, though? The situation was like a triple edged sword. Walking away meant giving up the opportunity of a life time. Staying meant continuing to be the bullies' punching bag, and then there was Dad, my staunch and loyal supporter, to face.

No matter which way I looked at it, the fact was that I was sick and tired of being bullied and wasn't going to put up with it any more. It was the hardest decision I had ever made at that point in my life.

I tried as best I could to keep my ear out for phone calls on the house phone because I knew at some point Dean would call, as he always spoke to either of my parents before and after a game. I didn't want my dad, especially, to answer or access the voice mail.

Plus the club had strict rules. Mess around and they had no qualms about releasing a player from the team, so I was not surprised to hear from Dennis about a week later. I was home alone when the phone rang. I let it go to voicemail. 'Kostas we have not heard from you. Come down and have a chat with us so we know what is going on.'

Three days later, I met him in the car park at the training ground. After the normal pleasantries, I told him I wouldn't be returning. 'I have no passion for the sport any more, Dennis. I feel like I have out grown it.'

He was clearly disappointed, but at the same time he saw young people come and go and knew that many of them did not make it in the sport. He did, however, ask if I would reconsider, reminding me that it was the chance of a lifetime.

I repeated that my heart was not in it and I didn't want to waste anybody's time. I don't know which was harder, lying to him, or accepting the fact that once the words were out of my mouth, my hopes and dreams were over in that single conversation. There was no way back if I ever wanted to return.

I really wanted to open up to Dennis and tell him the truth as to why I was leaving. I couldn't. He would immediately get in touch with my dad and in my view it was the worst time for him to find out about my leaving the academy and being bullied, not only because he was headstrong about me becoming a footballer, but the bullies were not kids anymore. They were young teenagers who looked older than their age and my dad would probably handle them like men and do some serious harm to them. I didn't want that to happen.

It so happened that he left work early one afternoon and found me at home. 'Why are you not at football today?' he asked.

'It's a day off today,' I lied.

'There's a message on the phone,' he said as he picked up the receiver, tapped in the code and proceeded to listen to the message.

The expression on his face slowly changed and I silently pleaded, 'Please, don't let that message be from the club. Please let it be an old message.' I knew my plea was in vain when I saw the phone hit the floor across the room. How could I have missed it?

'What's wrong with you?' I asked, knowing full well why he was angry.

'How come you've left football?'

'I haven't left football,' I lied again. I wanted to be anywhere but there facing him at that moment. I wanted to get away.

'I haven't left football,' I repeated. 'I'm going tomorrow.'

'That's not what the message from Dean Holtham says. He said that you've quit. You ain't going back.'

I couldn't get out of this one, but I continued to lie. 'I don't love football anymore. I fell out of love with it. It's not what I want to do. It's not the path I want to take,' I gushed. It was the most difficult lie I ever told.

He went ballistic. 'That is absolute bullshit. How can you love it all these years and all of a sudden, you're out of love? That's ridiculous. You're going back. Call him back.'

I had worked unbelievably hard. In my mind, I didn't think there was a child that worked as hard as I did to get to the level I had achieved in football. It was my dream to be a pro footballer and my dad knew this. Everyone who knew me knew this. My dad, especially, had watched me come home every single day and play video after video of football matches. He watched me rewind and play, rewind and play, nonstop for hours and hours. He saw how determined I was. He watched me grow and develop as a player and saw that I had the right stuff to progress. So when he heard I quit, he just couldn't understand why.

To add, the word 'quit' was not in his vocabulary. Walking away from anything to him was just an impossible thought. Further, it was a sudden decision. He did not see any build up towards my decision and to say he was taking it badly would be putting it mildly.

I said, 'No, Dad, I don't want to go back.'

At that moment, my mum came in, asked what was going on and ended up arguing with him.

***

For an entire week, they had blistering rows and I was the cause of it. When Dad saw I wasn't going back, when it sunk in, he dismissed me and I became the disappointment in the family.

He did not acknowledge me. When I tried to joke with him he wouldn't blink an eye. He completely blanked me. I felt like I broke his heart and that broke my heart.

See, my dad was my world. My idol. You could say I was obsessed with him. I used to watch the way he walked and emulated him. I used to listen to the way he talked. I respected and looked up to him. There was nobody else I was connected to like I was to him. I liked his character and his ethics. I wanted everything about me to be like my father. He was, in short, everything I wanted to be. Perhaps it was because he was a successful figure and everybody wanted to talk to him and listen to him. I don't know, but it hurt me a great deal to see how I had the ability to disappoint and hurt somebody that I cared about so much. Never in my wildest dreams, did I realise I had the capacity to do that. It was unbearable to watch him.

His demeanor changed from then on. He stopped joking around, he was always in a bad temper and he became obsessed with cleaning. Also, I found out that a few of his business investments were not working out and he was facing a terrible financial battle. I killed the dream he had for me. A dream he was living through me because his boxing career was stopped at his peak, due to injury at age twenty-nine. So when I quit, something died inside of him.

As the months passed, Mum and Dad did not only show their disappointment. They voiced it and not only to me, but to complete strangers. On a daily basis Dad would tell me, 'You've ruined your life. You're going to be loser. You're going nowhere.'

On one occasion when I visited the café they owned, I sat at a table and my mum said to a customer, 'All of my children are successful. The only disappointment is him,' and she pointed to me.

I was so embarrassed. They were other people in earshot. And so it was that I was not only verbally abused and demeaned during my primary and junior school life, during my senior school years, during my footballing life, now it transferred over to my home life. It was a bitter pill to swallow, because these were people I loved, people I thought I could always turn to if I ever needed to tell them what was going on and get some comfort from them, but they turned on me as well in a way. They rejected me because I was not one of their successful children. I was a disappointment.

To add, the recession hit and hit hard. It affected them in a big way. Their three businesses, a chip shop, pizza shop and café were not doing well. The pressure was on as things went from bad to worse. My dad constantly flared up and lost his temper, with me in particular, arguing and running me down.

I was constantly reminded that, 'You've ruined your life. This was your one chance. Your life's over. You're going to be a loser.' And on numerous occasions he would say to me, 'You're going to be just a bin man. You're going to be picking up people's shit for the rest of your life and that's the life you're going to live.'

I didn't see anything wrong with being a bin man. It's a perfectly good job. However, it was draining listening to the one person whom I looked up to, whom I loved with all of my heart and whose opinion meant the world to me, lose faith in me. It was worse than any beatings or emotional or verbal abuse I took from the bullies at school and football and I soon found it impossible to live with him.

I was in emotional turmoil and became dependent on myself in the sense that I only relied upon my own thoughts, my own feelings and I had to find my own way of sorting things out. I didn't have anyone to turn to.

My emotions were stirred. How much more of this could I take? My presence was causing unnecessary misery. I felt like I was a burden to my family. They were going through a terrible struggle and as much as I was going through my own personal battle, I wanted to try and take the strain off them as much as possible,

Because I was around the business daily, I could see how their decline was affecting them and it was causing a huge barrier in their relationship and in their relationship with their children. I was very much aware of how they were slowly disconnecting from everybody due to the recession. They were struggling to make ends meet and were on the brink of losing everything they'd worked their whole lives for. I was in tune with what was going on and could see the pain they were going through, which is why I felt like an added burden. At that point, my thoughts were all over the place and I didn't know what I was going to do so I continued to live through the dysfunction.

I was heading indoors one day and was in an unusually positive mood when I saw my parents in their car which was parked on the driveway. They appeared to be arguing, probably about money, I thought. As I walked past them, my dad said something along the lines of, 'Have you got a job yet? What are you doing with your life?'

'I've just come back from an interview,' I told him.

'What are you going for an interview for?'

'Just an office job, trying to get some money to help out.'

'What's the point? You ain't going nowhere, you blew your chance. Football was your career and you blew it. You might as well just give up.'

It sounded to me like he was showing me the door, but I knew that deep down he didn't mean it. He'd just come out the back of an argument with Mum, was angry and frustrated. Dad was an incredibly giving person with a heart of gold, but he was on the brink of losing everything and lashing out. Unfortunately, I was in the line of fire. 'Whatever,' I retorted and walked into the house.

A few minutes later, they followed and whatever they were arguing about escalated and the argument continued. Riled up and in a temper, Dad turned to me and said, 'I think you'd better fucking sort your life out, because if you don't fucking sort your life out, you're going to end up on the streets like a tramp. We're all struggling. We can't survive.'

I could see the strain on his face. He was blaming himself for the problems and certain business decisions he'd made that didn't quite work out. I wanted to take as much strain off him as possible. I couldn't look him in the eye. I couldn't bear to see how he looked at me anymore. It was just too much.

Just like how the bullies broke my spirit, so did my Dad, and I thought, 'Enough is enough. I'm not going to take this anymore.'

My stubbornness kicked in, or maybe it was inner strength I didn't know I had. Whatever it was, I wasn't going to let anyone drag me down, even my own family. It just wasn't going to happen.

'Fair enough, if that's what you want. Now, this is what's going to happen.' I walked up the stairs and packed a small suitcase, the size of a carryon and thought, if I walk out that door there is no way I'm taking a step back in. I've got to go out there and sort my life out.

I took his words on board, 'Go out and sort your life out. If I were you, I'd go out there and I'd fight for my life to make things happen. I wouldn't quit. I wouldn't be a loser. I wouldn't give up just the way you have.'

I closed the suitcase, 'I'm going to fight on my own.'

Chapter 7

OFF THE BEATEN PATH

'Be the change that you wish to see in the world.'
— *Mahatma Gandhi*

THE DRIVEWAY WAS long and as I walked along it, I glanced back and thought, 'I'm never going to stay another night in there again. This is it.'

I continued walking away from the only home I ever knew. And I felt a change come over me, like I was transitioning into another me – a new me and within this new me I felt a burning fight, a rebellious fight. I was going to prove my parents wrong and in my head I told them: 'There's no way I'm going to be a nobody. I'm going to show you and I'm going to show you my way; you and no one else are going to tell me that I'm a loser. You have no right to tell me I'm going to be a nobody because you don't know who I am inside. You're my parents, but you obviously don't know me well enough. If you did, you'd know that I'm made of better stuff than that.'

After my inner bantering, I found myself walking in the direction of my Greek grandfather's house. I was halfway there when I stopped as a thought struck me. My dad goes there on a daily basis. If he sees me there he would think that I was freeloading off of my granddad. I imagined the look he'd give me. That look alone would be enough to make me feel rubbish about myself. I couldn't go there.

I changed direction and walked for hours around the area. It eventually grew dark and I needed to find somewhere to sleep. I went over to my mate, Tony's house. He lived on the other side of an abandoned building with his sister. I explained to him that I had nowhere to stay and asked, 'Have you got any room for me?'

'No, mate, there're kids here.'

'Okay, Tony. No problem,' I told him like it was no big deal, but I was screwed with nowhere to sleep. However, my pride kicked in. I wasn't going to beg anybody for anything.

I headed toward the abandoned building that was across the way and not far from my granddad's house. It was boarded up and plastered with graffiti over the outside walls. Drug addicts hung around outside and I saw a ripped up sofa by the porch with needles scattered over it. Someone said, 'Who the fuck is this?' I ignored the question, since it wasn't directed at me and walked between a couple of addicts, entered and looked around.

There were used condoms on the floor, women's personal things strewn around. Everything bad that could be crammed into one building was there. It was a building of pure corruption. I had entered hell.

My heart raced fast because I was just a kid who didn't really know much. I went through a lot of rubbish through school, but I had never seen filth and obscenity to this extent. At seventeen-years-old, I didn't have an ounce of street smarts in me.

The building had three floors. I gathered my wits and walked through the first door that led to a hallway, where there were stairs leading to the next floor with a room to the left. I walked into the room. A body lay flat out on the floor out cold from drugs. There were needles by her side.

I chose to stay on the ground floor because if the building caught fire, I could get out before it burnt to the ground. There was a half broken door to the right of where I stood, I pushed it open and walked in. The only thing in sight was a ripped up sofa and an old dirty torn up mattress. I looked at it and thought, is this going to be my life now?

My heart raced double time. I had seen movies and television shows about homeless people. I never would have thought that I would ever be in such a position, but I was. I was homeless.

I looked through the only window in the room. Gangs stood and sat around injecting themselves with drugs, others shouted at each other. In the distance, two men were punching the living daylights out of each other surrounded by cans of beer on the ground. What an absolute nightmare! Could I survive through the night?

I looked at the floor. There were maggots and creepy crawlies crawling around. My eyes moved to the mattress. I was scared to go near it, much less lie on it. I didn't want to think what nasty germs were concealed in it. The entire surrounding was noisy, disgusting and I was disgusted, but I had no other place to go and I was extremely tired from hours of walking, as well as sleepy.

I folded the mattress, braced it against the wall, placed my clothes over it and sat upright with my head resting against the wall. I knew I wasn't going to get a wink of sleep that night, with people arguing, shouting, laughing inside and out, doors being opened and slammed at intervals and people walking up and down the stairs all the time. Not only that, I couldn't risk sleeping as anyone could access the room and God knows what they would do to me. I was an easy target. It could be the end for me. Tonight could be the end of my life.

I sat thinking for hours, what can I do to prove my parents wrong? What path shall I choose to become successful?

Chapter 8

THE FRIENDSHIP FACTOR

'Well, limbo is not a good place to be.'

— *Bill Joy*

I LAY AWAKE most of the night, forcing myself not to nod off, but sleep eventually overcame me. At some point in the early hours of the morning I jumped awake, expecting to be lying in my nice warm bed at home, in my nice neighbourhood. It took me a few seconds to recognise where I was and when I did; it was like waking up in a dark, misty horrible nightmare.

In daylight, the filthy condition of the room was magnified and I was absolutely petrified. My insides felt empty – not lack of food empty.

I had to get out of there, wash myself and get my day started so I headed back to Tony's house and asked him if I could use his shower. He said yes.

Afterwards, I walked to the shopping center in Kings Heath where I asked every shop owner if they had any vacancy, some did, but required a postal address for application purposes. I no longer had one.

With no joy finding a job, I walked around looking for an alternative place to sleep and came up empty.

I was tired lugging my stuff around, so I headed back to my friend and hung around with him until it grew dark. When he said, 'Kos, I am going to head in now,' my heart sank. I was going to be alone.

Back in the same room at the abandoned building, I took in my surroundings proper. The walls were bare. Holes in it told me someone had punched it in a fit of anger. Any wallpaper it had was long since torn off, replaced with graffiti. On one side the words, 'I love so and so,' was evident. Seeing this gave me a strange, yet nice feeling. It showed me that once upon a time normal people lived here with children.

In contrast, on another wall, there was graffiti of another kind. Gang names such as, PFT which stood for Pool Farm Troopers then my eyes caught the words 'HELP' written in tiny scribble. Reading it sent shivers down my spine and I wondered if I wrote it the previous night while in an unaware state. The initials, 'R.I.P. J' were also etched on the wall.

It dawned on me that this place was a place of pain, a place for tortured souls that had lost their way in life. This was their place of self-destruction until they either ended up in prison, became drug addicts, or even worse, dead.

The place reminded me of the film 'Titanic,' starring Leonardo Di Caprio and Kate Winslet. Before the ship sunk, it was full of life and laughter. After, it was a broken vessel of suffering and death. That was what the dilapidated building reminded me of, those who had drowned in their self-destruction.

The dominating thought rummaging through my mind

was how to get out of the situation I was in. The second wasn't so much a thought per se, but more a prayer. I held my mobile phone in my hand and prayed the position I interviewed for would pan out and I'd get the job. That would solve my problem in a snap. When it got to around 7 p.m., logic told me the call wasn't coming.

The darkness made the place scarier and my nerves were on edge. I pretended I was somewhere else and played games on my phone. About 10 p.m. I was in the middle of playing 'Snake' when I heard someone creeping towards my room. My heart raced, but I stood up, walked to the door and pulled it open. As I did, somebody sprinted off. I closed the door, laid down on the torn up mattress and curled into the foetus position like a scared child, while shaking like a nervous wreck. When would my fortune change?

That night I probably slept for about two hours on and off as I kept checking for daylight. As soon as daybreak appeared, I felt safer. I stood up and immediately felt weak and off balance. For a second I thought I was going to collapse, but I pulled myself together. It was the side effects of lack of food and sleep.

By 6 a.m. I was roaming the streets. The morning air was fresh, which made me feel human. The sun was rising and I thought it doesn't matter where you live and how terrible your area is, if you want to see something beautiful, wake up early and watch the sun rise.

After walking for about an hour, I began to feel cold so I returned to the room, not that it was much warmer, but being indoors helped somewhat. I thought of ways to get my next meal and the only solution was my granddad. At around 9 a.m. I walked over to spy to see if my dad's car was there. It wasn't. I ran over and knocked on a window.

'Yea?' he shouted.

'Granddad, it's me, Kustagi,' I said, using my Greek name

by which he called me. He passed me the key through the window and I let myself in.

Granddad was a funny character, plus his English was terrible and you couldn't help laughing when he spoke. He was always so pleased to see me and that made me feel good, because he was about the only person at this stage that was happy to see me.

After about ten minutes chatting with him, I said, 'Granddad, is it okay if I have a look in your fridge for something to eat? I'm hungry.'

'Of course,' he said.

I rummaged through his fridge like a wild animal. He ate a lot of frozen chicken and beef curries; I picked up a chicken curry and heated it up in the microwave. I had never been so excited to eat a frozen meal before. It tasted so good.

We sat talking as normal and though he was looking at me, he didn't see what was happening to me and I was bursting to cry out to him for help, but I didn't.

I felt people should be able to see my pain without me having to tell them and having to ask for help, so naïve was I.

By the time I returned to the building, it was fairly dark. I slumped onto the mattress. However, I could not relax due to the creaks and scary noises that ranged from screaming and laughter from the drug addicts in the other part of the building.

Not long after, I heard someone in a distressed voice repeating, 'Please no, please no, Coward man is sorry.' His repetition was doing my head in. I went to see where he was. He stood outside looking towards the top of the building, which looked like it had been burnt. The exterior wall was black.

I walked back to my room, confused yet satisfied that

he was a crazy harmless man, but I couldn't get settled and constantly got up to check outside the room to see if any intruders were lurking around.

After a while, I nodded off only to be awakened by massive banging. I gathered my senses and the banging became louder. BANG, BANG, BANG, 'Open the fucking door! Open the fucking door before I torch this whole place down!' someone yelled.

My heart palpitated so hard I could feel the pulse beating in my temples. I snuck to the door and peeked out to see a guy kicking another door. He held what looked like a butcher's knife, as he stumbled left and right. He was clearly drugged up or drunk.

The kicking and shouting went on for about an hour until he left screaming at the top of his lungs, 'I am going to burn this fucking building to the ground tonight. You're all dead!'

I sat with my hoodie covering my face rocking back and forth for a long while thinking, why me? Why did this have to happen to me? I worked myself up into such a temper, tears flooded my eyes and I yelled the loudest scream I have ever done, 'Fucking why?' As I shouted and screamed, I heard people laughing, as if they were laughing at me.

***

The following day, I walked aimlessly around and as I passed people on the street, I made eye contact with them, willing them with my mind to help me in some way, just help me. In fact, I was pleading. I was hoping they could read my desperation and in my desperation I started playing mind games.

I met Tony around mid-morning and he said, 'Kos, you look terrible, mate. Your eyes are bloodshot, you're pale and you look really fragile. Come on. Come with me.'

His sister was out so he took me to her flat. I took a shower and he gave me some clothes to wear and told me to get an hour's sleep on the sofa. Before I did, I told him about the night's antics and asked him if he knew who Coward man was.

'Yeah,' he said. 'Coward man's family used to live in the abandoned building where you are staying. One night, there was a huge fire in the upstairs flat. Coward man jumped out of the window not realising his family was still inside.

'When he heard his children screaming, he tried to run back into the flat to rescue them, but the flames were too powerful. He kept on trying until the screams stopped. His brother-in-law came after he heard about the incident and beat up Coward man, repeatedly saying to him, 'You're a coward man, you're a coward man!'

'The story goes that when Coward man stood up from that beating, the shock of the whole situation made him snap and ever since, he walked around shouting, 'Coward man is sorry, Coward man is sorry.'

'After that, the building seemed to be a place of torment. I've only ever known bad things to come from there.'

After he told me the story, I lay on the sofa thinking about Coward man's sad experience, and how he let somebody's opinion define who he'd become. I was worried I was going to do the same thing.

I fell asleep shortly after. When I woke up, it felt like the best sleep I'd ever had. Tony told me I was crying in my sleep and laughed at me then said, 'C'mon.'

'Where are we going?'

'My treat, just follow me.'

We hopped on a bus that took us to the city center.

I felt alive seeing people walking around in suits. I admired people who wore suits and promised myself that I would be like that person one day, dressed in a suit.

Everyone seemed so normal. I craved some normality in my life.

We walked from the city center onto Hagley Road and whilst walking Tony said, 'Kos, what's happening with you man? You never quit, but you're living your life now like a victim. Why don't you make a plan to get out of this situation and start to have a life again even if that means going back to your parents?'

'Mate, every day I think about how I can get out of my situation, but I would rather battle my way out of the torture I am feeling than play a part in killing the two people I love the most.'

'What do you mean?'

'Me being at home was killing my parents due to the stress I seemed to cause them. I can't bear to see the look of disappointment on Dad's face anymore.'

'In that case then, I'll make a deal with you. The food and drink my sister throws out because it is a little out of date, I'll put in a bag. Two days a week come to the shop and collect it. If some weeks there aren't any, I'll give you some from the shop, okay? But I'll only do this under two conditions. One is you come to the gym with me three times a week to start to get your confidence up and feeling strong again. Two, start pushing yourself to find a way out of this situation, man.'

'Cheers mate.'

'C'mon, you've always had a champion's way of thinking; now it's time to bring that champ out.'

I felt motivated and empowered, and was still hoping I'd get that telephone call about the job, but that feeling slowly died, along with getting the job, as my third night turned into a fourth, fifth, sixth... before I knew it, it was take each day as it comes. With each day, the situation grew worse and worse because I had no money, which meant I had no food apart from Wednesday's and Friday's when I met up with Tony, plus my only mode of transportation was my own two feet.

Though I got a lot of help from my friend, he could not change my life for me. No one's going to be able to do that. I've got to fight for myself and stop looking to the outside world to give me something or provide for me. I had to build my own life, but I was in limbo. I had no solid plan apart from getting through each day with the thought process that, 'something had to give.'

Chapter 9

IMPROVISE, ADAPT, OVERCOME

'Life never goes as planned...it's in those moments where you define yourself adapt and overcome. You'll become a better person because of it.'

— *Unknown*

WITHIN A WEEK of being in the building, my survival instincts rose to the surface and I was on alert. This was not a game. This was my life and I had to protect it.

Though I got off easily the first few nights without any major disturbance, I began to feel like a target due to the awkward glances from people, some of whom walked into the room any time during the day and night. My fear heightened after observing a few drug addicts befriend a young lad about my age, they engaged him in conversation and laughter then kicked the living daylights out of him until he ended up in a coma.

I was already under a lot of mental strain and my mind was conceiving all sorts of negative things and ran rampage with thoughts of, these addicts are going to kill me after taking drugs. They would befriend me then harm me.

Whenever I walked into the building and one of them threw me a friendly nod, I thought he was plotting to kill me.

Switching rooms didn't help. After three drug addicts walked in on one occasion, I felt even more unsafe and the fact that it was on the top floor increased my angst, because I was further concerned that I would be trapped if there was another fire. I snuck out of the fire door and returned to the original room. I made it my room, my territory and I was going to protect it.

Tony got me a lock, which didn't do much. From time to time, it was broken off and evidence that an intruder entered my room was that of my mattress turned upside down or syringes on the floor.

I devised a ruse, whereby, whenever I sensed someone outside my door, I growled at the top of my voice, 'WHO THE FUCK IS OUTSIDE MY ROOM!' and punched the wall. I figured if I act crazy, if I behaved like a wild animal they would keep their distance and my Incredible Hulk-like actions would give my space a level of protection.

When I wasn't stuck in the room playing games on my phone, I spent most of my time hanging out with Tony when he was free. I grew to hate hearing the words, 'Kos, I am going to head in now.' It signalled that I would be alone and it was torture. Sometimes, I lingered on creating pointless conversation just to have his company for a little bit longer.

I kept my word and started going to the gym with him regularly. I did not have to pay to become a member, because Tony knew the owner and asked him if I could go to spot him, which wasn't the case. The owner saw me using the equipment many times, but because he remembered my dad from his boxing days, he let me off.

I found a lot of comfort talking to Tony. Even though he wasn't in my situation, he had a level of understanding. We joked about it sometimes and would shoot the breeze to pass the time. He always checked in as to whether I was keeping up my end of the bargain, which was keep myself mentally strong so that I did not slip into a weak way of thinking by letting my homeless circumstances destroy me.

Unfortunately, I did fall into that way of life. I became in some ways a product of my environment and began to behave differently, including being aggressive.

I had been living in the building for around four months when things took a turn in my circumstances. Tony's sister found out he was giving me food and told him that if he continued she would kick him out. I was then only getting bits and bobs off him when I went to the food shop where he worked.

I started to frequent a local chip shop every Saturday around midnight. I'd charmed the owner or cracked jokes and he would sometimes give me any remaining food they were going to throw out.

Then his hours at work increased and he couldn't attend the gym three times a week any more. As a consequence, my visits became irregular.

One night I looked around the room and asked myself for the hundredth time, 'How did I end up here?' I got off the mattress for whatever reason and though it was dark, I caught my reflection in the dirty window and was horrified at what I saw.

My homeless life style showed through my wiry, fragile skeletal body, gaunt face with baggy eyes and dark shadows around them framed by long and scraggy hair stared back at me. I did not recognise myself.

I peered into my eyes and saw the child who just wanted acceptance and approval. I felt ashamed then felt sorry for me and wanted to hug myself. Before I could, a burning determination erupted in my stomach and the fighter in me said, 'NO, NO WAY AM I GOING TO ACCEPT THIS IN MY LIFE!'

It seemed to me that God was giving me inner strength to make the changes needed to change my life. I needed to get physically strong again. When I am healthy, I felt strong internally, too.

There and then, in the dirty bedroom, I started doing pushups and sit-ups. I punched the brick wall to toughen up my knuckles until they bled. In a sick way, it helped to release all the pent up emotions that resided inside of me.

I did not generally hang around the area in the daytime. It was bad enough sleeping in a place that was infested with drugs, crime and sometimes death. If I stayed around, I would eventually become an addict, or get involved in crime. It was the last thing I wanted. Plus, there were many gangs that loitered about. But since my decision to get fit, I needed to get out without being recognised or invite any kind of contact.

Luckily, it was the autumn season, so I developed a swagger, wore my hoodie over my head, wrapped a scarf to shield my face revealing only my eyes and jogged around the neighbourhood for hours then returned to my room and worked out like a mad man.

I was heading to my room one day when I smelt burning. It faded after a while so I continued, only to find a man standing inside staring at the wall. Before I could ask him what he was doing there, he slit his wrist. Shocked, I dived on top of him. I didn't want to see him kill himself, especially on my watch. The knife fell out of his hand and landed on the floor.

He began to scream at the top of his lungs. It was such a torturous scream it raised the hairs on my hands. His eyes rolled in his head from distress. Angry and worked up because I was scared, I grabbed hold of him and shouted, 'What the fuck are you doing?'

'I want to die. I want to die. Get off me. I've had enough. I want to just end it all,' he shouted.

I imagined he was off his head on drugs, or going through withdrawal. The knife was close to him. I leaned over, picked it up and threw it out of his reach. It landed underneath the old dirty sofa.

'Just calm down, you don't want to do this,' I said and grabbed hold of his clothes and lifted him to his feet. I felt strong, but then again I was dealing with someone who was skinny, fragile and weak. It was really a false sense of security, because I was scared and didn't trust him. Yet, another part of me felt really sorry for him.

He reached out to me in an aggressive way and I pushed him away. 'This isn't the way. You don't have to do this. Sort yourself out,' I told him and threw him out of the room. 'Don't ever fucking come up on my patch again,' I shouted and immediately my heart sank for treating him like that, but I had to. He was acting unpredictable and I had to man-handle him. Plus, the next time he takes his bout of drugs, he may come to hurt me, instead of hurting himself. I needed to send some kind of fear into him and maybe he would tell his friends that I was no pushover.

***

About two weeks after the incident, it was throwing it down, along with thunder and lightning and I was hurrying along, walking in a straight direction towards the building when I saw the man who tried to kill himself to my right, heading on a different path, though close to where I walked.

He took his top off, growled like a beast and walked toward me. I tried to avoid him, but he caught up and stood in front of me raking his nails across his chest. Evil flashed in his eyes.

'I'm going to slit your throat and I'm going to throw you in the canal,' he said, referring to a ditch that was beyond some bushes. He then pointed to a little girl who was walking with her mum and said, 'What do you expect when I have to look at that?'

What he was saying made no sense to me. He was obviously high on drugs, but I was shook up. He looked like he would do some serious harm, whether to himself, or to somebody else.

I grabbed him by his shirt and threw him against the gate. 'If you ever approach me again, I'm going to do exactly what you said you'd do to me, to you.' I let him go and he scoffed off into the distance.

I continued to see him hanging around the building completely off his head on drugs. He was not unusual. Many of the other people who lived in the building were addicts, too. I became accustomed to seeing needles on the floor; someone leaned up against the door of the room I slept in or in a corner, or the stairs. Somebody always had a needle stuck in their arm, or already off their head.

I couldn't avoid them and at some stage I developed an arm's length relationship with a few of them, meaning we would have a conversation at times, but I wouldn't allow anyone to get too close to me, because I didn't trust them.

A few of them admitted that they'd committed murders and they'd do it again and they were proud of it. Their reasons were because it was revenge, or they were under the influence of drugs.

Chapter 10

TRADITION AND ENCOUNTERS

'Do what you can, with what you have, where you are.'

— *Theodore Roosevelt*

ALONG WITH BECOMING fit, I wanted to do something constructive and searched around my mind as to what I could do with my limited education, and without money, to make a life for myself.

When I played football at Birmingham City Football Club Academy, I attended a football coaching scheme, with the objective that if I didn't make it as a pro footballer, I could get a job coaching. It was a scheme that was available to all team members. Given that I quit the academy, I didn't finish the course so coaching was out of the question.

Plus, I genuinely fell out of love with the sport, as I subconsciously associated my negative experiences with football. There were times when I considered rejoining a team, but I felt sick at the thought, so much so that I couldn't even kick the ball. I just did not want to be near one and didn't watch any football matches. I kept as far away from the game as possible.

I thought about my dad's story. His parents were Greek Cypriots, who used to live in a small village in Cyprus before immigrating to London. My granddad was a bit of a jack the lad. He worked multiple jobs and was very smart and had a taste for gambling.

Like my dad, he, too, had a temper and a reputation in the Greek community for being tough. He was not the kind of man to take rubbish from anyone. He later took up weightlifting and became a British Weightlifting Champion in 1966.

Granddad moved around a lot to evade debtors chasing him for money he'd borrowed and gambled away. He eventually settled in Birkenhead just outside of Liverpool. At the time, Birkenhead was not deemed a safe neighbourhood. However, Granddad spent a lot of his time with his Greek friends gambling and getting up to all sorts.

One day, he had a bet with a friend that he could drink a whole bottle of whiskey in one go. After he downed the liquor, he froze for about a minute before collapsing from a massive stroke. He was thirty-seven-years-old.

He survived the stroke, but it left him crippled for the rest of his life. Outside of his shine for gambling, he was an extraordinary person who lived to the age of eighty-seven, spending more of his life disabled than he did as an able bodied man. Still, Granddad apparently had about seventeen different near-death experiences and survived them all.

My dad was about eleven-years-old when he moved to Birkenhead. By the time he was eighteen, he was getting into trouble, sometimes with the law and his mother was concerned for his safety. She sent him off to Birmingham to live with an uncle. At first, he struggled to settle in the city and continued to get into trouble.

However, not long after, he saw my mum working at a shop along a bridge in a little kiosk. He approached her and asked her out on a date. The story goes that she said, no, because she was busy that weekend. Dad didn't give up, he said, 'How about the week after?' She agreed and he stood her up twice before he took her on a date.

It was at that point that he made a decision to turn his life around to get on the straight path. Dad held a lot of resentment at that time towards Granddad because he gambled everything away. Nevertheless, he was already an amateur boxer by the time he'd moved to Birmingham, so he joined a local boxing gym.

Mum told him, 'If you're going to get punched, why not get some money from it and go professional?'

He did, and at the age of twenty-five, became the British Welterweight Boxing Champion.

They married the same year he won the title and soon after started a family. Dad was smart with his money and whilst boxing professionally, bought a business and a house to raise his family and several other businesses thereafter.

***

That's a possible route I could take, I thought. I could become a boxer... carry on the tradition. I placed that thought on hold and questioned, 'Who do I idolise? Who do I want to be like? What can I do without money?'

The answer was easy. I idolised my dad. I always wanted to be like him and boxing didn't require any upfront money. I made an instant decision to go for it. But how would I get to the gym? It was all the way in Birmingham City center, miles away. Boxing might not require money, but travelling did.

I would walk. Once I made the decision, I couldn't wait to get started walking and when I did, it was like walking from under a black cloud into the sunlight, because I was walking away from a place of filth and nothingness. I was walking to Birmingham City Center, where there were people who were happy, or seemed happy. They were people who were well-dressed, not dressed like the down-and-out bums I saw on a daily basis. I had removed myself so far away from normal people, that I was amazed when I walked past someone in the street who was wearing a suit. He looked really sharp and I smiled at him. I felt excited. It was the strangest thing and as crazy as it may sound, it felt like a privilege to be next to him and I said, 'Wow! One day I want to look like that in a suit.'

I was in a good mood by the time I got to the gym and as I entered, I felt some self-worth. I started to feel like somebody again.

John Peg, the head coach at the gym looked me up and down and asked, 'Who are you?'

'Kostas,' I replied.

'That's funny. There used to be a champion called Kostas.'

'Yeah, the champion you're referring to is my dad,' I told him while scoping out the gym. My eyes caught a picture of my dad on the far wall. I felt a sense of pride that guys were training and my dad's picture was there for all to see, and I'm his son. The son of a highly regarded figure in the boxing world and I felt like I'd come home. Instantly, I knew this place was where I belonged. This was where I wanted to be.

'You're Kostas Petrou's son? You're the Greek Tank's son?' John asked as if confirming.

'That's me,' I said proudly.

He said something to the effect that I was lying, not in a, 'I don't believe you,' way, more as in, 'You're shitting me.'

But I retorted, 'No, I'm not lying.' I had a picture of me and Dad on my phone and I showed him. 'Look this is my dad and this is how he looks now. He hasn't got hair anymore,' I laughed.

He smiled and said, 'Your dad was an absolute warrior, they used to call him 'The Greek Tank.' He shouted over to one of the other men in the gym, 'Lenny, come over here and meet the son of The Greek Tank.'

I felt such a sense of pride and for once in a very long time, appreciated.

As Lenny walked towards us, John said, 'I am going to introduce you to Lenny Woodall, the father of Richie Woodall, former World Champion.'

When Lenny joined us, he told him, 'This is Kostas Petrou's son.'

Lenny shook my hand and said, 'What's your name?'

'Kostas,' I told him, 'same as my dad.'

'How is he, still training?'

'Yeah, he goes to the gym all the time, still super fit.'

'What a tough man he was. You know, he was a throwback, if they made them now-a-days with the same heart your dad had, we would have a lot more world champions. So what brings you here then? You want to be a fighter?' he asked.

'I think so.' In that moment I wondered, how the hell did I go from being around a bunch of druggies who have nothing in life, took drugs and hurt themselves and other people, to being in the presence of one of the most respected boxing trainers in the U.K and being treated like a special person?

'Okay then kid, your dad was great. There's every chance you ain't never going to be as good as him, but let's see what you've got.'

'Fair enough, that's fine.'

He gave me a pair of boxing gloves. I put them on. There

were two boxers training in the ring and he told them, 'You guys get out of there. Kostas Petrou is stepping into the ring now.'

Well, did my ego swell, or did my ego swell and I cockily thought, 'Yeah, that's right.' As I got in the ring, Lenny said, 'So do you know the basic punches and what they mean?'

'Yes, I think so.'

'Okay, so I will shout out combinations and from time to time I will say move your head and you need to duck or bob and weave to avoid my shots coming back at you.'

'Okay,' I said.

I had no technique, but I hit the pads. With three-minutes to show off my stuff, I punched the pads and as I got into momentum, everything around me went silent. Everything seemed to stop and I realised how much pent up anger I had inside of me and I wanted to pour it all out through the gloves. My eyes focused on the two hands holding the pads and the fury in me raged and I wanted to knock those hands off. I put all the power I had into the next punch and blasted the pad. It leaped out of Lenny's hand and landed outside of the ring.

I noticed that everyone, including the other coaches, stopped what they were doing and all eyes were watching me.

Lenny pulled me to the side and said, 'I've been training champions. I've been training a lot of people, but I've never in my life come across somebody with such raw natural power. If you hit somebody like how you just did, that will be it. If you stick around, kid, you're going to become world champion one day.'

I didn't expect that reaction from him. It just kept getting better and better. My confidence went through the roof hearing those words from someone who trained world champions. He had to know what a world champion pedigree looked like and in his eyes and experience, I had a chance. I felt like I was stronger than everyone in the gym. I felt like bloody King Kong at that moment.

His statement sealed the deal for me. I was going to be a boxer, but first, I had a score to settle.

Chapter 11

REMEMBER ME?

Revenge is a confession of pain.

— Latin Proverb

I SPENT CHRISTMAS and New Year practically alone for the first time in my life, apart from the time I spent with Tony. I was living in the building for about six months at this point and became hardened to my surroundings. Nothing shocked me anymore.

To add, things got worse, as more drunks and addicts hung out in the area and I saw things that in my opinion, no young person should ever see. Even though I had turned eighteen, I was still a young man. I saw men, women and children get beaten to a pulp. Many times, I intervened.

I interceded on one occasion when I heard arguing between a well-known druggie and another man. Their voices were deafening so I went out to check what was going on. As I got there, the well-known druggie pulled a knife out and stabbed the other man in the torso and ran off. I sprinted over to him, took my scarf off and tightened it around his wound to stop the bleeding.

Someone must have called emergency, because an ambulance pulled up about ten minutes later and took him to the hospital.

I did not get further involved or asked any questions, in case people thought I was connected to the man. I was street smart by then and knew that if I asked one person if he survived, he most probably knew the druggie who stabbed him. Word would get to him that I was asking questions, he would come knocking at my door asking me why I wanted to know about the stab victim; then I would become a target.

I saw violence and pain on a near-daily basis and slowly, I lost feelings and my sincere emotions died. My mindset changed and so did my way of thinking.

As time passed me by, I desperately wanted to get out of my dire living situation and thought long and hard about how to find a way out. I also became bitter and resentful and wanted revenge; revenge for the situation I was in due to the bullying I experienced. If it wasn't for those bullies, I would still be following my football dream and not be living in a rat infested dump. They were going to pay for killing my dream.

I already knew where some of them lived and those who I didn't know, I would track down and inflict the same pain they inflicted on me. I wasn't a fragile, weakling anymore. I wasn't scared of them anymore. I had grown over the last few months even though I wasn't eating very much and my physique had changed due to the workouts at the gym. My body looked similar to what my dad's used to look like; my arms were muscular and I was lean with a six-pack.

***

It was dark and cold though it was early spring when I left the gym one evening. During the walk back to the building, my mind was like spaghetti junction. Thoughts were filtering in all directions and by the time I reached the room, I sat down weary and angry on the dirty mattress. The positive thoughts I felt a few hours earlier had all but dissipated.

I sat there for some time and the longer I sat; the angrier I grew until it seemed to be bubbling inside my chest. I sprung off the mattress and snatched it up. An insect shot out from it and landed on my arm. I threw it against the wall, shouting, 'No more. This is it. I'm not scared of anything no more.'

My insides seemed to open up. I felt like I was breaking free of something and the mattress was symbolic of this freeing moment.

I turned it over and in my mind it was as if in doing so, I was turning my life over. I flipped it over again and said, 'This is it now. I'm flipping everything around. Everything that's been done to me is going to be undone.'

I am going to go out there and fight to become somebody, because I knew I had something special in me. I have to go out and find it, but first and foremost, I was going to get the bullies. They were not going to get away with what they did to me.

The mattress was almost ripped to shreds by the time I was finished flipping it over and over. I put my clothes back over it, sat down and began to plot how I was going to get the bastards.

My mind flashed back to an incident at school: A girl had been sick over the bannister of some stairs I happened to be walking down. I didn't know this at the time, until one of the bullies, the ringleader, grabbed me at the back of my neck and pressed my face into the vomit, smearing it all over. My glasses hung around my nose. I, too, wanted to puke, but ran to the toilet and washed my face, trying not to cry. I couldn't help it and burst into tears. As I ran, the bully shouted, 'Run to the toilet like the little Greek dickhead you are,' and laughed.

Disgust filled my being as I relived the disgusting and humiliating moment and I said, 'I know where you live.'

He didn't live far from the abandoned building. I had spotted him once or twice at a distance over the months. I got up and walked the five minutes it took to get to his house to scope it out. I wanted to find an area where I could jump him without being seen. His house was at the end of a street and beyond, led to an alleyway that was surrounded by bushes and a couple of rundown walls. Perfect.

I spent days watching out for him and purposely walked in that direction hoping that one day I would bump into him.

I played a scenario in my head constantly about what I would do when I encounter the bullies and I was so consumed with getting back at them that everything else in my life didn't mean anything anymore. My life was already ruined. I was living in a dump because of them.

I could not move on unless I conquered that part of my life. A career in boxing was all very exciting, yeah. I gained some confidence from the one gym session I had, but the sugary words that Lenny fed me didn't ring through anymore. The moment had passed. After so many years of having no confidence, one gym session wasn't going to change that. I didn't believe it. I still felt like a nobody and my life was going nowhere. I didn't care if I killed him. I'd be better off spending time in prison than live in squalor for the rest of my life.

My tactics of walking past the bully's house finally paid off. It was a semi-dark night when I saw him leave. I watched him as he walked down the path towards the alleyway and I sprinted round the back so I could ambush him at the other end. I got there before he was even half way and hid between some bushes and a wall that had the word 'Death' scrawled over it. I was taken aback and wondered if it was a sign. For a moment, I had second thoughts about going through with my vengefulness, until I saw his figure getting closer and all my resentment resurfaced.

When he reached a couple of feet away from me, I stepped out in front of him and he stopped in his tracks. A look of fear crossed his face. I was dressed in a hoodie that covered my head and a balaclava. We had not crossed paths or seen each other face-to-face since I quit football.

Standing in front of him, I felt a cocktail of emotions, the most prominent being anger. I was so worked up I actually felt myself wanting to cry, but as I looked into his eyes, he seemed to be shrinking, I seemed to be growing and before me I saw a stupid kid and actually felt compassion for him.

It was almost laughable looking at someone I used to be scared of, who at the time appeared bigger than what he was; now I was no longer scared of him, he appeared smaller.

I pulled my hoodie off my head aggressively, plucked the balaclava from my face and said to him, 'Remember me?'

It took him no more than a couple of seconds to register recognition and he acknowledged me with a smirk on his face. 'Look here, it's the Greek bastard.' His hands were down by his side, obviously not expecting me to attack him.

I threw the first punch with every single ounce of my body weight behind it and hit him with a straight right flush on the chin and heard an echo like a clapping sound.

When I was training for those brief moments in the gym with Lenny, he pointed out certain parts of the body to hit when boxing. And he followed with, 'When you hit your opponent, come in at a downward motion so you catch him downwards.' I was evidently a quick learner, because it was the same technique I used on the bully and he dropped like a sack of spuds to the ground. I caught him completely off guard and he lay there unconscious. My punch knocked him out cold.

I was initially going to warn him and walk away, but his facial expression looking fearless and hearing is cocky remark when he saw me aroused the memories of all the things he'd put me through. I grew angrier and leaned over and laid into him with a barrage of punches, shouting, 'I'm here because of you, you bastard. You've ruined my life.' I kept saying it over and over and punching him over and over, while he lay on the ground.

Reality hit me and I became conscious that I had to stop or I'd kill him. I was sweating, my heart was pounding and it felt like it was going to explode. I wanted to cause him more damage, but I abruptly stopped and walked away; then I remembered the pain he caused me when he thumped me the stomach at school and I crawled into the staff room thinking I was going to die. It was one of the worst pain I'd ever felt. I thought, you put me through that and I didn't deserve it. I'd done nothing to you. All I ever wanted was to get along with everybody.

I ran back and booted him in his stomach like a football. I wanted him to feel the same pain he'd inflicted on me.

He did not react. I didn't care, though for a split second, I thought I'd caused serious damage. I turned and ran, and ran, and ran.

I returned to the room and sat on the mattress. 'What have I done?' I felt absolutely awful and remorseful for my actions.

I brooded for a little while then it dawned on me that I could actually look after myself. Why didn't I do it before? I didn't feel good about it; neither did I feel bad about it. I felt completely empty, because I'd seen these scenarios happen around me for the last six months and I'd become immune to it. The only difference was that I was now a part of it.

Now, for the next victim.

Chapter 12

PUTTING THE PAST
TO REST

*'Instead of a man of peace and love, I have become a
man of violence and revenge.'*

— *Hiawatha*

FROM A YOUNG age, I watched movies starring one of the most influential martial artists of all time, Bruce Lee. His fantastic martial arts skills made an impression on me and I dreamed of being like him. Apart from admiring his finesse of minimal movements and extreme speed that had maximum effect on his opponents, I was always drawn to what he stood for: defending someone, or someone's honour.

I rationalised that I was defending my honour... I was defending myself and so I got the majority of the bullies in different, yet similar ways, though the first one got the worst beating.

It wasn't easy tracking them all down, but I was much

more street smart than when I left home, and was able to devise crafty ways of setting up scenarios to catch them.

One bully in particular, who was my next target, was rather slippery; he was always in a public place. One day, while I was with Tony, I saw him. I asked Tony to lure him by offering him some cigarettes. He did, but to get them he'd have to go to the shop, they had to walk down an alleyway to get there. I jumped him. My modus operandi when I approached a bully was always the same. Hoodie covering my head, a balaclava and I'd ask, 'Remember me?' before I beat the shit out of them.

While I was exacting revenge, I had begun training at the boxing gym on a more consistent basis, so my physique was powerful, my body was stronger and so was my confidence and reputation, which unfortunately was not in a good way. I was fearless and didn't think twice about fighting anyone, no matter how big or how old.

My reputation grew so bad that people were skeptical to approach me, including my friends and family. Even Tony's sister didn't want to come near me.

I was on two paths that were going hand in hand. In my personal life, I was tracking people down and taking revenge; in my boxing life I trained in the ring and they both bounced off each other. I carried the anger from the street to the gym and the training from the gym to the street.

Due to my training, I was able to predict people's reactions from their body movements - what they were going to do before they did it so I was able to slip left or right, dodge punches or put people down by utilizing certain punches depending on the situation. To the average Joe, it was fun to watch. The guys in the area who knew me began making jokes about my tough-guy image and started calling me Rocky, among other names.

Fun as it was to watch, I did not enjoy getting revenge. I did not enjoy being a hoodlum, as my surroundings dictated. I did not enjoy those dark moments. After I hurt and got my revenge on the bullies, I crawled back to my room and tears would roll down my face because the truth was, I am not a vindictive individual and I never wanted to hurt anybody.

On the other hand, I was torn between two worlds and felt the only way I could move on with my life was by putting my past to sleep and that meant revenge. I had to get even with the bullies to get it out of my system even with sorrow in my heart.

Nevertheless, on a separate occasion, the brother of one of the guys who used to bully me and whom had been one of my victims had recently been released from prison after serving time for apparently killing someone. He sent the word out that he was going to kill me.

Interestingly, the night before I heard about his threat, we got into an altercation. I was walking along the street when a car pulled up beside me with tinted windows, which powered down as it rolled slowly along the road. As I looked into the vehicle, a group of guys pretended to shoot me using their fingers in the shape of guns.

I walked up to the car, leaned my head through the window and said, 'If you're going to fucking kill me, get out the car and do it like a man. Line up. Line up one by one. Every single one of you, line up one by one and I'll take you all.'

I was at the point where I didn't care what anyone did to me. I wasn't backing down anymore. I'd put up with enough threats and bullying in my life. It was a case of when you push a man so far, when his back is against the wall, he's going to lash out and now I had no qualms about lashing out at anyone, even a bunch of stupid idiots who were trying to act clever. They looked at me like I was crazy and sped off.

I never saw them again.

***

A few weeks later, I met Tony at his place of work; we embraced, happy to see each other. After catching up on each other's lives, the topic of one of his sister came up.

'It's her birthday today, man, but I'm working late. I won't be able to drop off her present.' he said.

'What did you get her?'

'Just a gym pass and a card,' he paused then asked, 'what you up to today?'

'Not a lot, swimming with the sharks,' I laughed.

'Would you do me a favor, if I give you a fiver, would you drop it off to her?'

'Sure.'

'Tell her I'm working late, but I'll be down in the next couple of days to see her.'

'Of course, but you don't have to pay me to do it.' Even though five pounds was food for at least three days, it was the least I could do. Tony had done, and did so much for me.

'No, no, take the fiver, its fine.'

'Thanks mate.'

It was around 1p.m. when I started the three mile journey to Maypole where Tony's sister lived. As I approached an alley way close to her house I noticed three guys, one leaned against the right of the wall and the other two on the left. They wore hoodies that covered their heads. As I got closer to them, I smelled weed - nothing unusual in that area. My instincts, however, sensed danger and I was aware that if they jumped me, I could only go forward or backwards.

I continued walking and as I passed between then, a hand landed across my chest. 'What you got in your hand?' the owner of the hand asked, nodding towards the envelope in my hand.

'Get your hand off me pal and let me walk on!' I said in a stern tone. Before I knew it, a fist connected to the side of my head. My reflexes kicked in and I turned towards him and punched him once with a right hand that sent him to the ground. The other two simultaneously threw punches at me; I ducked and grabbed the left hand of one of them. At the same time, the guy on the ground got up and I grabbed him and held them at arms' reach, the other one shuffled around me and I felt something graze my arm.

I looked down and saw a big gash. I turned towards him only to see him aiming a knife at my chest. My heart pounded. He wasn't satisfied that he'd stabbed me, he wanted to kill me! All the shit I'd been through raced through my mind and I asked myself, 'How much do I want to stay alive and what do I need to do to make that happen?'

Despite all the crap, I wanted to live. I stepped back and punched his hand with all my might. The knife landed on the ground and I picked it up before he knew what happened. 'Come on, come on, I'll rip you all to shreds, you scum bags!' The face of one of the guys turned yellow from fright and they scampered off. It all seemed to happen in a split second.

I looked at my arm again. It was pouring with blood and seeing the outpour shook me up and I felt unsteady. I picked up the envelope that had fallen on the ground during the scuffle and made my way in the direction of the abandoned building, glancing around in case they came back to finish me off.

My eyes caught sight of graffiti on one side of the wall that said, it does not matter what has happened in your life up until this point, what matters is, what you are going to do about it!

It was a message. It had to be. I paused at the profundity of it then reflected; okay, so I got verbally abused in primary school, I got physically and verbally bullied in secondary school, my dream of being a pro footballer was scared out of me and I am homeless, living in squalor, so what am I going to do about it? Play victim and act like a defeatist, or fight for my life like the champion I know I am?

Chapter 13

PUT TO THE TEST

'Nothing great was ever achieved without enthusiasm.'

— *Ralph Waldo Emerson*

I THREW MYSELF into training at the gym and got to the point where I was sparring with professional boxers who were preparing for championship fights. They were at the top of their game. I was also learning a lot of life lessons from the sport and other people.

During a training session one day, I got talking to an Indian lad who was also training. He came across pretty wise, and at one stage during the conversation he asked, 'Have you ever used your boxing on the street?'

'Of course, all the time, nobody messes with me.'

'You know, it takes more strength to walk away than it does to stand up and fight.'

'Yeah, but if some idiot tries to make a mug out of me then of course I'm going to lash out,' I retorted.

'Well, if that is how you feel then carry on, but remember what Gandhi said, 'An eye for and eye, and the world goes blind."

His response made me pause and I laughed awkwardly. I had no response to such a powerful statement. 'Catch you soon,' was all I came up with and walked off.

I never saw him at the gym again.

Later, John Peg said to me,' Jump in the ring with Mart.'

Mart was preparing for a British title fight and was known for being tough, strong and was a heavier weight than me, not to mention much bigger.

'Take it easy on him!' John shouted to Mart.

Take it easy on me! He had no idea what was happening in my life and his statement stirred the wrong emotion within me. No one's taking it easy on me. I've never had it easy so no one's going to take it easy on me in the ring either.

I felt angry at the thought that somebody should give me a break, illogical as the thought sounded in my head, I didn't want that. Don't give me a break.

No sooner did I climb into the ring; Mart came at me with a look that said, 'I'm going to wipe you out.' I felt that he wanted to prove a point because I was Kostas Petrou's son.

He hit me with everything but the kitchen sink. One huge right hand landed flush on my chin. It did not phase me. I realised then that I could take a good shot. I felt the impact, of course, but it didn't affect me in any way. I thought, 'Okay, give me your best,' and he did. He pounded away at me and gave it all in the first minute. Someone mumbled, 'Ohhh, Kostas is getting kicked, like getting knocked out!'

The other boxers begun to crowd around the ring, at the same time Mart landed a shot on my face that made a 'Foom' sound and everybody chorused, 'Ooh.'

They were like animals wanting blood and kept repeating, 'Go on Mart. Knock him out.'

The punches kept coming but I felt nothing. Listening to the other's reactions, I could tell they thought I was in pain and was about to go down.

Out of nowhere, an internal strength from within rose to the surface and I sunk into a punch, really, really sunk into it and hit him into his body with a right hook. He gasped!

My adrenalin was flowing and for the second time, I learned something about myself. I was tough. I had powerful inner and outer strength. To still be standing in the ring after a battering from a potential champion sealed that for me and I went all out on him.

I hit him about seven to eight times in a row, left, right, left, right. I pushed him away from me and hit him with one almighty right hand and his legs danced, wobbling like jelly.

I was ready to knock him clean out with best my shot, a left hook. I got into a stance on my big powerful legs. He was wide open and as I was about to hit him, John, screamed, 'Time! That's it. That's it now. That's it.'

Afterwards, Mart came up to me and said, 'My sinuses were playing up. My sinuses were playing up.'

And I cockily replied, 'To be honest, my knuckles were playing up as well. He walked away and I saw his body shaking with laughter.

I felt good. I always needed reassurance about my ability and I knew after that sparring match, I had what it took to be a boxer and that became my new dream. It was the path I was going to take in life. I was going to be a professional boxer.

I remembered Lenny Woodall telling me the first time we met that I could be world champion one day. I wanted to make that a reality. I approached him and asked what I needed to do to get there.

He looked at me and said, 'Your dad was great, but I'm telling you now, you're greater. I know that because I watched your dad. I know how good he was. You are rare. Don't let this opportunity go, because you've got so much natural ability.'

'You just shook up a guy who has never been stopped in the ring, so that goes to show your ability.'

I sat in a stupor listening to him and found what he was telling me amazing because my dad was my idol.

Lenny then told me that Richie Woodhall's son was coming to the gym the following week to take a look at me and also do some training with me. I could not believe it. I was going to be training with a legend. Richie was also Team GB boxing coach, which meant that he clearly was the top boxing coach in the UK.

I was enthusiastic about meeting and proving myself to Richie and trained unbelievably hard during the week running up to his arrival. I woke up extra early, jogged then trained for longer periods at the gym with the intention of making a good impression.

I pushed myself so hard that the night before Richie was due to visit I developed a fever, my body hurt when I inhaled and I started to hallucinate. Regardless of how ill I felt, I was not going to let this chance slip away from me.

Richie turned up around 6 p.m. and everybody flocked around him while I shadow boxed, down playing my excitement. About five minutes later, Lenny approached the ring and said, 'Rich, I want you to meet Kostas, the lad I told you about and the son of Kostas Petrou.'

Richie hopped into the ring. 'Kostas, great to meet you, I remember your dad very well. I hear you're not too bad yourself.'

I froze for a minute, not only from the excitement of finally meeting Richie, or standing before him face-to-face,

I still felt unwell and weak. But I would be damned if I was going to reveal that. I put on a strong persona and said, 'I'm okay.'

'My dad says you have a cracking left hook,' he started to put on punching pads, 'Let's see what you've got then.'

I lowered my head and closed my eyes. 'This is it, time to show up.'

He shouted combinations: 'Throw and Jab, straight right hand, left hook, duck and follow up with a straight right, left hook....'

I knew the combinations like the back of my hand and loved them. With each follow through from his, instructions he repeated, 'Good, good, very good.'

Finally, I threw a combination so crisp that when I landed the final left hook, the pad flew off his hand. He picked it up and was visibly excited.

'Throw that combo, again,' he instructed.

I did and the sound from the power of my punches echoed throughout the gym, bringing everyone to a standstill. However, I knew I could hit harder if I was fully fit. At that moment, I was on the verge of collapsing but stood tall.

'Well, I can certainly see what my dad was talking about when he told me about you. Your power is phenomenal,' he told me and ended the session.

I felt on top of the world hearing those words and knew for sure that boxing was my ticket to success. This was my way from obscurity to a life of my dreams. Plus, everyone in the gym heard those words come from the lips of Richie Woodhall, a boxing hero.

After everyone settled down, Richie pulled me to one side and said, 'Kostas, I am going to tell John and Lenny to set up a training plan for you. If you follow this plan religiously and take this career one hundred percent serious, you could be world champion because you have all the tools to do it, you have talent that I have not seen in a very long time, if at all.

'For now, though, I want you to start training and focus on participating at the London 2012 Olympics. I want you to follow this plan and in four months I'll come back to see how you are coming along and get you to spar with one of the lads who will be boxing at the Olympics.

'We'll see how you handle yourself against him. If you do well, I'll give you every chance to represent Team GB.'

A legend in the sport believed I have the skills and talent to become world champion, but even more to the point, I could be boxing in one of the biggest sporting events ever!

I was completely blown away and all but smiled, nodded and agreed to work his plan. 'Thank you for showing faith in me. I won't let you down,' I told him as I fought back the tears that threatened to spill. He had no idea what that meant to me.

I walked back to the abandoned building on a high even though I felt drained.

Chapter 14

WORKING THE PLAN

'We all have dreams. But in order to make dreams come into reality, it takes an awful lot of determination, dedication, self-discipline, and effort.'

— *Jesse Owens*

A T 5 A.M. every morning, I got up and ran 4 miles, exceeding the limit on the plan and 8 miles, sometimes. I was the first to enter the gym barring the person who opened it and the last to leave. Sometimes I hid in the toilets until the gym was locked up and slept in the boxing ring. I ensured I woke up early, hid in the toilets again until the gym opened and began training.

Boxing became my main focus and I practiced the same punches over and over, whether at the gym or in my room; in fact, at every opportune moment. I also trained my mind to become the best in the profession to a point of obsession. Before I knew it, I was easily beating top-rated and talented boxers in the country.

My physique was a far cry from the scrawny weakling I saw in my reflection a few months before. It was now muscular and my upper body resembled that of my father at his peak, though my thighs and legs were huge, unlike his. They aided me to carry out powerful knockout punches and I used them to my advantage.

About two months into my training, Jon, one of the coaches from the gym, invited me to a dinner show. Guests included boxing legends Frank Bruno and Steve Collins. Later into the evening, Steve interviewed Frank and they exchanged banter, though I could see there was mutual respect between them. At the end of the interview, guests were allowed to meet and talk to them. I capitalized on the opportunity and joined the queue to speak to Frank. When I finally got to him, he politely said, 'How you doing?'

'Pleasure to meet you, Frank, I'm a huge fan. Just wondering if you wouldn't mind telling me what you think of my training schedule.'

'Yeah, go for it.'

I outlined the whole program and he listened intently. After, he said, 'You really train like that?'

'Yeah, why?'

He laughed his hearty trademark laugh and said, 'You're training for my world title aren't you, kid? World champions train like that so if that's what you want to become then keep it up.' He shook my hand.

Everything was falling into place. Even world champions respected my work ethic and I could feel a huge transition was about to happen in my life.

I followed Richie's plan religiously and by the third month, I was like a fighting machine. I was also training with Elaine, a French Olympic coach who started working at the gym. He felt I had huge potential and spent hours with me every day.

***

Richie came to the gym on a Thursday, along with a Team GB boxer from my weight which was welterweight. I felt ready to show him how I improved, though my heart was pounding.

After warming up, Richie signalled it was time to go into the ring. Elaine placed the head guard on my head, slid the my mouth piece into my mouth, rubbed Vaseline over my head guard so that punches would slip off, rather than my head catching the full impact and smeared some over my face for the same reason.

During the first round, I was nervous and the Team GB boxer caught me with some good shots, making me feel a little bit out of my depth. It ended with him out-boxing me.

As we rested between the rounds, I started getting flashbacks of the area I was living in, the pain and suffering I was going through living like an animal and I told myself that his guy is the one person standing in my way between continuing to live in squalor or creating a better life. A surge of power sailed through my body.

I was ready for round two. I threw two quick solid jabs that made his head pop back and another with the same result. He responded with a jab and a right hand that I anticipated, I ducked, shifted to my left and hit him with a sickening left hook to his ribs and followed up with a right hook to his head. He flew through the ropes and out of the ring. It was one of the best punches of my life and a move that I had been practicing for months.

He was conscious but shook up. He then started being sick in a bucket as a result of the body punch. I jumped out of the ring and went over to him to make sure he was okay.

Richie came up to me after everything calmed down and said, 'Kostas, you've improved more than I thought you would. You really are a natural born fighter. I want you to go for a medical and let's get you ready for the Olympics.'

I literally leapt up and down from joy and excitement. When I calmed down, I shook his hand.

I walked back to the abandoned building feeling on top of the world; my life was going to change, finally. I was going to represent England at London 2012 Olympics and my new goal was to win gold!

Chapter 15

A POKE IN THE EYE

'Everything is okay in the end, if it's not okay, then it's not the end.'

— *Unknown*

CHASING A DREAM can be tough. I quickly learnt that it takes perseverance–more perseverance than I've ever had to muster in the past. Chasing a dream was stretching me in ways I've never been stretched. I had to work on my mental strength to stay committed and disciplined and I began to feel like I was actually becoming a different person as I pursued the goal of becoming Olympic champion and professional boxer.

But I enjoyed being stretched and continued my training program until it was time to visit the optometrist for my eye examination that is standard procedure all boxers have to go through as part of a full medical, which I believe the World Boxing Federation medical board recommends.

After the test procedure, the optometrist looked at a folder I assumed housed information about the history of my eyes. 'So Kostas,' he began, 'you had an operation on your right eye when you were…,' he glanced at the folder, 'very young, around… 5-years-old.'

I wasn't sure if he was asking me a question or making a statement.

'It seems as if that operation was slightly successful, but not to the point we would have hoped for,' he continued with a worried look on his face. 'The sight in your right eye is very poor and your left eye is making up for the weakness. Unfortunately, with your eyes the way they are, I cannot pass this medical.'

I didn't quite understand what he was saying, but was pretty sure it could be fixed. 'Okay,' I said slowly, 'so just sort me out with laser treatment or whatever it is they can do nowadays to fix people's eyes.'

'Kostas,' he said with a sad look on his face, 'let me explain the situation with your eye. The problem you have is that your right eye does not connect properly to the visual cortex of your brain, which resulted in amblyopia, or what is commonly known as lazy eye. The only chance you had of fixing this problem was when you were a child, which would have required you to wear a patch. If it's not treated then, when you get to a certain age, the problem is unfixable. Unfortunately, you have reached a certain age.'

The problem was unfixable! I dropped my head in my hands. After a few seconds, I said, 'So with all the technology we have nowadays you cannot save my life by fixing my eyes?'

I didn't expect him to understand what I meant by saving my life, but it was crystal clear to me—if boxing was taken away from me I had nothing left to aspire to anymore, nothing to focus on and without a focus, a man is just being. We are not here on earth just to be, we are here to see out our purpose and my purpose was boxing.

'Kostas, I am so sorry. If there was something I could do I would do it, but there isn't at this stage in your life, you'll have to play with the hand you were dealt.'

Deflated, I stormed out of the room. I felt as if a huge piece of me was stolen. No! Ripped out, and I had no way of getting it back.

I walked straight to the gym, found John and said, 'Can we go and sit somewhere? I really need to talk to you.'

I was shaking. If John couldn't help me, this was the end of my way out of my shitty life.

Before he could say anything, I rumbled on, 'John, I went for my eye exam, and he failed me. He said because of my eye problem it can never be fixed and he couldn't pass it.'

Like me, he was gutted. Placing his arm around my shoulders, he said, 'Kos, sometimes in life we think we are on the path that we are destined for and that we have found our life purpose, but we do not know what the bigger plan is. Somewhere along the line, there is a bigger plan for you, but it does not involve boxing.'

'How can that be? I'm a natural at this sport. This is like my bread and butter and now someone is just taking it all away from me. What am I supposed to do?' I said in despair.

'Kostas, I know this is hard, but I want to explain something to you.' He looked deep into my eyes as if looking for my soul. 'Before you are born, there are up to one billion swimmers trying to make it into this world, you are one in one billion, and sometimes even more.

'You were the strongest, the fastest and the most determined. You were a champion over one billion. Now, I believe that you were the one for a reason. I also believe we all have a purpose on this earth and we are not just one in a billion by chance.'

He paused, and then continued. 'Let's face it, if you were one in a billion in any other walk of life, you would be a champion in your profession. You thought boxing was the profession for you, but clearly there is another plan.

'My advice to you, kid, is this; take all the determination, all of the pain and struggle, all of the heart, desire and hard work and all of you and go find your path, then apply all the qualities I just mentioned and focus them on your real destiny.

'One day, when you find your destiny you will turn back and say, 'now I know why being born with a dodgy eye was more of a blessing than a curse; because that is the reason I am here today."

My mind was telling me that John meant well with his philosophical words, but they did nothing to ease my disappointment. I was well and truly gutted. My head was all over the place. I couldn't come to terms with the fact that my boxing dream was over just like that.

I thanked him for all his help and told him I would still be around.

Chapter 16

TURNING POINT

'Quiet the mind, and the soul will speak.'
— *Ma Jaya Sati Bhagavati*

THE EMPTINESS I felt was so overwhelming it filled my whole body as I walked the long walk back to the abandoned building. I had many such journeys before, but this was the loneliest ever.

What now? I kept asking myself. How do I find a way out of this one? I am stuck without any money, any food, any education, no career, still homeless and nothing to aspire to.

When I got to my room, I sat in a stupor and sobbed. The night passed into day, into the next and into the next. At intervals, I pressed my bad eye into my head, hoping it would miraculously connect with my brain in the correct way. I was so desperate.

About week of doing nothing but sleeping, crying and taking the odd walk, I was sitting in my room one mid-afternoon wallowing in self-pity, when I heard someone shouting, 'Kostas, Kostas, come quick! Come quick!'

I casually got up, annoyed with life and angry with whoever was interrupting my pity-party. When I got to the door, a girl I'd seen a few times, but had never spoken to, stood outside crying. 'What do you want?' I asked.

'Its… its… its Tony,' she stuttered.

'What about Tony? And why the hell are you crying like a baby?'

'He's dead, he's dead.'

'What do you mean he's dead, you stupid crazy cow!'

'He's been killed. He's been stabbed…' she stopped. She was crying so hard she could hardly talk.

It was only then I realised what she was telling me. I was so blinded by my own pain and sadness I hardly registered what she said and when I did, it hit me so deep, I felt as if a bomb exploded in my heart and the chemical it released was pain.

She pointed toward a fence, between a patch of grass and pavement. I sprinted over to see if she was telling the truth. By the time I got there, the area was cordoned off and the police seemed to be everywhere. I looked down and saw a puddle of my friend's blood.

I ran forward shouting, 'No! No!' A police officer held me back. I wrestled with him and four others joined him and held me down.

When I settled down, they let me go and I ran and ran and ran. I did not know where I was going, but I ran until I could no more. I wanted to run away from everything. I wanted to run to a different planet where I did not have to suffer any more.

Exhausted, I eventually fell to the ground and punched the grass repeatedly, shouting, 'Why? Why? Why?' I begged the ground to swallow me up.

Tony was my best friend, the one person who truly saw my suffering and who truly knew my heart because he saw my pain. He gave me money in times of need, trained with me, snuck food to me when he could, gave me words of encouragement when I was down and made me feel human in a very inhuman environment. Now he was gone. Some stupid idiot took away my best friend and I had to live with the pain of his loss.

I felt more lost than I ever had before.

As I cried for my friend, I remembered a poem Muhammad Ali recited by Helen Steiner Rice, on the Michael Parkinson show:

Beauty of Our Friendship

Friendship is a Priceless Gift
that cannot be bought or sold,
But its value is far greater
than a mountain made of Gold.
For gold is cold and lifeless,
it can neither see nor hear
And in the time of trouble
it is powerless to cheer—
it has no ears to listen
Nor heart to understand,
It cannot bring you comfort
or reach out a helping hand
So when you ask God for a gift
be thankful if HE sends
not diamonds, pearls or riches
But The Love of Real True Friends.

And a true friend he was. So often I said to myself, right now I need Tony more than he needs me, but one day when I am successful, I will give him all he ever wants as a thank you for being there for me when I was lost. Now, I'll never get the opportunity to repay his kindness.

After a while, I got up and walked to the hospital. When I saw his body, I felt I lost a brother. Life would never be the same without him and I knew that on special days in my future I would always think of him and speak to him to let him know that he is with me always, in memory and in heart. I prayed for him.

After, I sat in the chapel talking to God. I asked him over and over to change my fate and over and over I kept hearing in my head: to change your destination you first need to change your path.

Hours later, sad and disillusioned, I walked back to my room. When I entered, I caught my reflection in the murky window and saw a broken man. Tony was so right. This was a building of suffering. I had somehow slipped into that category.

I lay down and fell asleep. At intervals, I woke up from the sound of my screams. This continued for many nights. Occasionally, I heard someone creep into the room; I did not budge. My heart did not race anymore, I simply did not care.

After two weeks of what could only be described as self-imposed solitary confinement, I had the sudden urge to get out of the room and go for a stroll.

As I walked out the room, I almost stumbled over a drug addict who lay outside the door. As I went to pass him he said, 'Oi, you, why don't you stick this needle in your arm and make all that screaming go away?'

I looked at him. It was so easy to quit my dismal life and take drugs, but no matter what challenges presented itself, an old saying always came top of mind: I would rather die on my feet, than live on my knees.

If I gave into drugs I would just be living on my knees. Giving up on the pressures of life by taking hits, rather than standing tall and taking life's hits, I'd prefer to die a fighter than a quitter.

'Let me ask you a question,' I said to him, 'how far would you go to get your fix?'

'Sometimes thirty miles each way,' he replied.

He seemed fairly straight and sober, which surprised me, considering he had a needle right next to him.

'How much effort and risk do you go to, to get your fix?'

'You know, sometimes I go to hell and back to get my fix, sometimes I risk my life to get my fix,' he responded in a sincere tone.

'Change what you're addicted to and one day you won't be lying in the hallway of an abandoned building trying to get young people hooked on drugs, but with your determination you will be on top of your profession teaching them how to become successful.'

I felt so broken over losing my friend, and in general, I wanted to lash out or be lashed at, as warped and sick as the latter thought sounded in my head. Instead, words of wisdom sprung from my mouth. It was like something, or someone else had spoken through me. I was just the presenter of the words.

I dismissed him and walked out the building.

Chapter 17

BROKEN BRIDGES REBUILT

'Our behavior toward each other is the strangest, most unpredictable and most unaccountable of all the phenomena with which we are obliged to live. In all of nature, there is nothing so threatening to humanity as humanity itself'

— *Lewis Thomas*

O NCE OUTSIDE, I had the sudden urge to visit my parents. It would be the first time since leaving home. As far as they knew, I was staying with a friend and we'd usually meet either at my granddad's house, public places, or talk on the phone. I preferred to keep them at arms-length.

But I needed a diversion to get me out of the stalemate zone that kept me on lockdown, even if it was negative energy. And if anyone could produce that, my amazing parents, who had always been there for me and whom I loved more than anything else in the world, were ahead of the queue. They'd remind me what a disappointment I was.

I wasn't going to prove them right, though. I would rather die on my feet than live on my knees, whether in an abandoned building or not. My stubbornness wouldn't allow it. I had to figure things out by myself.

I ran my fingers through my hair and straightened my clothes using a window as a makeshift mirror, to ensure I looked presentable. My appearance alone would show them I was doing okay and that was all they needed to know.

Satisfied with the result, I headed in the direction of their house. I made a conscious decision not to tell them what had happened to Tony; they would find out through the grape vine eventually. I was protective of everything and anything, even my pain. I did not want advice on how to deal with it, I did not want any sympathy; I would deal with it my own way even if that meant going in a tortuous environment.

I smiled at and said hello to everyone I passed to pump up and get me in an upbeat mood. As I got nearer to the house, I saw a neighbor walking his dog. It was Lawrence, aka LOL. It wasn't only easier to refer to him using the acronym, but befitting, because he made us kids LOL.

As he neared me, he smiled and I all but started to cry, I felt so emotional. Seeing him brought back memories of my beautiful childhood.

Growing up from a young age, he was a constant sight walking his dog. Sometimes, he gave me 50p to buy sweets and called me little spark, because I never could stay still.

How amazing is life, I mused, in a short period, my world turned upside down and I have gone through every emotion a human being can go through -- granted, it was of my own doing, yet this old fella is on his same journey and life seems to be steady for him.

Somehow, I stifled my tears.

He was delighted to see me, as I him, and asked how I

was getting on, what was I up to and went on to say how fast I had grown. He remembered me as a little kid with big glasses and always energetic. If only he knew how worn out with life and physically drained of energy I was.

As we parted, he said four words to me that gave me the pick-up I was looking for, 'Never lose that spark.' I was rattled and headed to a quiet backstreet, sat on a wall and wailed like a new-born baby uncontrollably for about ten minutes non-stop. My whole body shook to its core. LOL brought to surface my childhood. I was back in a life where everything was innocent and beautiful.

After I calmed down, I continued to my parents' house. Mum answered the door and greeted me with a loving hug. A faint feeling came over me as we embraced, my legs turned to jelly and I felt on the verge of collapse as if I was punch drunk. I quickly regained my composure. The last thing I wanted was to collapse in Mum's arms.

We walked me into the house and the smell of breakfast tantalized my nostrils. My stomach expanded and I felt like a wild animal that couldn't wait to rip into his prey. She said she would cook me the full works.

Dad was surprised, but happy to see me. He placed his arm around me and we headed into the living room, while he asked how I was and what I was up to.

Here was my get out of jail free card, I could tell Dad about my dismal situation and be back home in a flash. I looked at the bigger picture and realised that if I went back to doing what I had always done, I would just keep on getting what I always got. Instead of using it, I said, 'I'm doing great, Dad. I have my ups and downs, but I'm on the right track.'

'You know I am always here for you, don't you? No matter what, you're my son and I will always love you.'

The flood gates threatened to explode again. It's so very easy to act strong and be strong when you feel strong, but it takes a true champion to stand strong when every cell in his body is crumbling. Man up!

'I know, Dad, and I'm here for you all, too,' I said, portraying strength, while repeating in my mind, pain is just weakness leaving the body, pain is just weakness leaving the body, pain is just weakness leaving the body.

The conversation turned to the economy. The UK had slid back into recession, the last time being in 2009, and my parents businesses were one of many that got hit and they couldn't seem to get back on an even keel.

I looked at my dad. They say eyes are the mirror of the soul. He'd aged over the last few months. The vibrant man I remembered who used to be full of energy looked like life was breaking him down, too. We were similar. We put on an exterior of, I can handle anything, but deep under the surface, we had levels of weakness and sometimes got lost. I would never have noticed the pain in Dad's eyes had I not experienced having my back against a wall.

I reached over and placed my arm around him. 'Dad, you are the Tank, remember what the commentator said in his commentary about your fight, 'This man is incredible the way he can come back from the brink of defeat,' well here you are on the brink of defeat and it's time to come back like you have always done.'

My words had the effect I intended them to have. His body language changed and he said, 'I will always fight on, son, no matter what.'

I felt we had bridged a gap in our relationship. Chatting with him felt like how we used to be.

Mum announced that breakfast was ready. It was a full English breakfast that consisted of two slices of bacon, two eggs, two sausages, tomatoes, fried bread, bread and butter, hash brown and black pudding. I attacked it with gusto and cleaned the plate.

After, we all sat together joking around. George and I teased each other like we used to. 'So skinny dude, how're things? You met any girls lately?' I asked him. We each had nicknames for each other. I called him skinny dude because he was thin and he called me, chunky dude due to my stocky build.

'Of course, chunky dude, you know my style,' he replied cockily.

We all engaged in casual conversation during the course of the day and later watched family videos. Being with my family was like a journey back to my childhood. Good times, like old times. A day I will cherish and remember for the rest of my life. A day I didn't want to end, but it had to. I felt like a prisoner who had a day release and it was now time to return to the dungeon.

'Right guys, I'm heading off now,' I told them, 'it was good seeing you all again.' We hugged and said our goodbyes.

***

I did not walk the route that would take me back to the abandoned building, I walked in the direction of Selly Oak, reflecting on what an enjoyable day it turned out to be, then I thought about my future and Tony, and how to deal with all that had happened.

The sun was getting ready to set in another part of the world, replaced by a nice breeze that made the atmosphere relaxing. Perhaps it was the calm before the storm. When I saw a bench, I sat down for a few and watched people as they went along with their daily lives, some rushed by, some on the phone laughing and chatting, or texting, while others strolled along.

Eventually, I got up and made my way toward the abandoned building. As I passed a newsagent that was next to the local job centre, someone shouted, 'Oi!' I turned in the direction of the big mouth and saw five lads, all of whom looked intoxicated. They weren't calling out to me. Again, he shouted, 'Oi, you, you sexy little slag!'

I looked around to see who they were shouting at and caught sight of a girl who glanced at them with a petrified look before shifting her attention elsewhere. Don't get involved; just walk on, every part of me warned.

Big mouth walked up to the girl, grabbed her bum and arm and pulled her towards the group that stood laughing by a footpath leading to a garden-like area between the newsagents and a shop.

'Lads, have you seen that huge fight down the road, it's all kicking off there, ambulances and everything,' I lied to distract them from the girl, who was now crying.

She looked at me and I became fired up with anger, but I had to be smart. There were five of them and one of me.

'Fuck off you dickhead! Don't come around here thinking you know what you're talking about.'

He was clearly off his rocker.

'Lads, shall we fucking kill this prick?' he asked his mates.

'If you think you're a tough guy then fight me one-on-one,' I looked him dead in the eye and told him.

The girl ran off and disappeared.

'Come on then,' big mouth said as he approached me. His friends formed a circle around us. He threw a punch that would have missed even if I stood still. I shifted to my right and hit him with a straight right. He was unconscious before he hit the floor.

His friends jumped on me, punching and kicking. Like a man possessed, I gave as good as I took, throwing punches at anyone. In the midst of it, I felt something sharp against my head. They all stopped and took a step back. I was confused. What happened? I, too, took a step back and looked at them and saw a knife with blood in the hand of one of them. Then it sunk in. He stabbed me in the head. I became aware that the white top I wore turned red as blood ran onto it.

My temper exploded and I saw red like the blood on my top. These guys were going to rape that girl and probably stab her afterwards, but instead it was me. I growled and charged at him. He wasn't going to get away with it.

He swung the knife; I ducked and hit him to the body and head with two lightning fast punches. The knife flicked out of his hand as he smashed against the wall. I grabbed it. I was cornered in the walkway, but now that I had the knife the others were scared to approach me. I backed out and shouted, 'Come on then you fucking cowards, you had to stab a man to win a fight, can't you do it with your own tools?'

At that point, the sound of police sirens interrupted us and I stuck the knife in my pocket, worried that if the police found my prints on it, I'd get into trouble.

The four ran in one direction and I ran in another, stopping only to throw the knife in a nearby bin outside of a shop. By the time I got to the entrance of Selly Oak hospital, I felt dizzy and off balance, barley making it to the wall of the entrance before I started swaying. Two nurses ran towards me and placed each of my arms over their shoulders and helped me into emergency, where I was taken straight into the treatment room. One of them checked my pupils to see if they reacted to the light. Satisfied I was not in imminent danger, they left me to wait for the doctor.

'What's your name?' he asked.

'Kostas Petrou.'

'What happened?'

'I don't know. I was running and in a second I was on the floor with blood all over me.'

He frowned and said, 'Kostas, I have been stitching up wounds most of my life, the wound to your head is a result of a sharp object coming into contact with your head. What really happened?'

I was scared he would call the police so I repeated, 'I just told you, I fell over. Am I going to need stitches?' I changed the subject.

'Yes, it is a very deep wound, not long but deep. I can actually see your skull, that's how deep it is.'

He put nine stitches in my head and told me to take it easy for a while. I headed back to the abandoned building. En route, I found a pound on the ground and used it for a bus ride instead of walking.

I was exhausted from the emotional roller-coaster of the past few hours and wanted the night to come to an end.

I rested my head on the chair in front of me until I got to my stop, walked the short distance to my room and threw myself onto the mattress.

Chapter 18

VISIONARY INTERVENTION

'Blessed are those with cracks in their broken heart because that is how the light gets in.'
— *Shannon L. Alder*

THOUGH I WAS bone-weary, sleep eluded me. I sat up with my back against the wall. A fusion of thoughts circulated through my head and I questioned how I allowed myself to become such a heinous person.

My actions of an eye for an eye and the world goes blind went against every grain of what I believed in. I went after the bullies, got my revenge, which ultimately proved to be pointless. My life hadn't changed. I'd lost sight of my sensibilities and had become barbaric, like them, thinking it was justice. The harsh reality was that I'd joined a vicious cycle that probably would never end.

Through my broodings, I heard the torturous screams of men and women who were either taking drugs, or had taken drugs fighting and slagging each other off. Glass smashed somewhere, doors slammed and the sound of a man's evil laughter travelled up to my room amid the wind blowing against the window. These were sounds I'd become immune to, but tonight, they were amplified.

I placed my hands over my face for what seemed like a second. When I removed them I was outside in a place I did not recognise that was foggy, dark and cold. Wind howled ferociously and whipped past my ears. I looked around; it was completely empty, no buildings - nothing.

I looked harder. The impression was that I was engulfed by a huge black cloud. It was the loneliest place I'd ever witnessed and I became confused, which was overtaken by fear and my thought was that I died and this was my fate, because I felt a sense of complete separation from life.

My legs moved and I walked into what looked like a never ending foggy path to nowhere. Yet, in the distance, I spotted rays of light beaming on the peak of a mountain and within me I heard, 'To get out of the black cloud you need to reach the rays of light at the peak of the mountain.'

There was no way I could climb that. It was too big, but I had no choice, I wanted to get out of this black cloud. I walked and walked and walked and when I reached the mountain I was intrigued, part of it was beautiful and crystal-like, the other, murky and muddy.

I started to climb. After a while, I was grateful to find a spot where I could sit and catch my breath, as I did, the figure of a man dressed in pair of black trousers and a black jumper appeared through the smog. He walked towards me and as he got closer I noticed his eyes were still and dark, but he looked friendly.

When he stood before me he said, 'Hi, my friend, are you lost?'

'To be quite honest, I haven't got a clue where I am. I somehow ended up here and about the only thing I do know is, I need to reach the top of the mountain to get out of here.'

He smiled, 'Right, okay, I can help you with that. I know a shortcut.'

'No, no, I'm okay, thanks. I'll carry on as I am,' I replied.

'Come on my friend, why struggle when you don't have to? Why go through this when you don't have to? Make it easy on yourself and take the short cut, it will make your climb a lot easier.'

For some reason I felt as if he was talking about my life rather than my walk to the top of the mountain.

'Fine, where is this miraculous short cut then?' I asked with a hint of sarcasm.

'Take the large path rather than the narrow one you were taking. It will lead to a road, follow it. You won't come out on the side where the rays are, but the other side. Trust me, though, you won't regret it. It is much faster and a nicer journey too, none of this hard rock stuff.'

He seemed genuine and so I went the way he recommended. I felt like I was flying. I eventually got to the road and jogged up the mountain side. After a while, it grew darker and foggier, soon it was pitch black and my next step sent me off the edge, tumbling down. My body banged left to right until I landed on the ground. Though battered and bruised, I stood up and realised I was back half way down the mountain. Worse, I could not see the large path.

Overcome by a mixer of physical and mental exhaustion with no will to go on anymore, I leaned my head against the wall of the mountain and cried out loud, 'I've had enough! I have had enough! Just let me fall.' Tears rolled down my face. I closed my eyes and urged myself to fall backwards and end it all.

A strong and powerful force took hold of my right arm. It felt familiar… comforting. I opened my eyes to see another figure of a man standing in front of me, his eyes pierced through mine.

'Nobody said it was going to be easy, they just said it is going to be worthwhile.'

He wore a white robe that ended at his ankles and his presence was overwhelming. Lost for words, I stared at him only to see my reflection in his eyes. My image was crystal clear. Clearer than any HD television, but half of me was dark, the other half, normal.

'That is why you need the rays at the top of the mountain,' he added as if answering my unspoken question as to why half of me was dark.

'The dark side represents you allowing yourself to become a product of your environment, thinking like the bad people you were surrounded by. In the process, you lost your morals and what you stood for. You used revenge as a way of feeling better about yourself rather than standing by them. It is easy to get angry, but it takes a stronger person to fight that anger and turn the other cheek.'

His words flowed through me, but I had already sussed that out. He wasn't telling me anything new.

'Remember, the only miracle formula in life is knowing that there isn't one.'

I found my voice, 'Surely there must be an easy way, a way that we all can learn what makes life simpler. Why do we need to struggle?'

'What good would it be to people if it was easy? We are not here to exist in a perfect world. This is a journey, and the best lessons in life are the ones you learn when you feel some kind of discomfort or pain. If it doesn't hurt, you wouldn't have a need big enough to make a change. Therefore, do not shy away from pain, embrace it, because your greatest growth will happen when pain and discomfort takes place.

'You have seen it written. Enter through the narrow

gate. For wide is the gate and broad is the ro
destruction, and many are fooled into believ
easy path and enter through it. This is the mis
made on this mountain. You took the large ⌐   ⌐ you
are being given a second chance.'

'Who are you?'

'Who I am is not important. What is important is who
are you? And more to the point, who do you, want to be?
We all have our own personal mountain to climb and it is
the journey to that mountain that shapes your character
and your life. Never jump in for the easiest and fastest route,
find the route that will teach you.

'To be successful in life, impact the lives of others in a
positive way. Go with an open heart. Be sensitive, gentle
and appreciative to others. Love, be humble and non-
judgmental. Use your willpower, courage, discipline,
determination, mental strength, faith and patience to help
you walk away when it would be easier to be involved in
conflict. Stand up for what is right.

'These are the characteristics you will need to be
successful in your life, now it is up to you to develop and
grow these traits. Stop looking for the fast and easy route,
stop complaining about the results of your own actions and
climb your mountain. Once you have, teach others how to
climb theirs.'

He disappeared into the fog.

I stayed rooted to the spot, his powerful words echoing
in my head and in an inexplicable way I felt as if I had been
reborn. I didn't want to fall off the mountain; I was ready to
take life head on.

I started to climb again; this time taking the rocky and
narrow route. I didn't actually believe I would make it to
the top. It was a painful and grueling ascent, but I was
not going to suffer just to survive, I was going to suffer to

succeed. When I felt at my weakest, the large path lit up, as if tempting me to deviate. I ignored it and continued, before long the pain my body was enduring became secondary as I seemed to develop an inner strength and I went harder, pushing myself beyond my limits.

At intervals, I looked up, searching for the light. Eventually, I saw it and felt a sense of achievement. I advanced and there I was, on the mountaintop standing before the rays of light, feeling the breeze blowing through my hands. Three steps took me into the light which absorbed my body, as if shining through to my deepest core.

I looked over the mountain. The rocky ground was replaced by a hologram and I saw myself as a young child surrounded by a glow, then being bullied - the pain was doubly powerful and I burst into tears; the glow started to diminish.

I'm a teenager being beaten up and the fire I carried for football was doused out. Thoughts of feeling sorry for the bullies; to wanting to help them to be better people; to hating and resenting them; to seeking revenge filled me, and the warmth from within became cold, dark and I disconnected from love of any kind.

I relived the hurt of being told I would amount to nothing and being a disappointment to my father. I felt his pain, too. To see me not fulfilling my potential hurt him, and increased when he watched me leave home, though he held strong.

I watched how I allowed thoughts of anger and revenge to override my positive thoughts. My morals and values went through the window as I assimilated and became a product of my environment.

A random moment of which I had no recollection appeared when I saw myself in church lighting a candle and placing it in the sand. Then its relevance became clear. The candle represents the light we need in life, we are all on a dark path and we walk around with our arms out in the air blindly trying to guide ourselves. We light a candle to light up the way to see the path. Sometimes the flame may blow out, but as long as you relight it, you will always be guided to the correct path.

I watched my boxing journey and fast realised why it was not the right path for me. I used it to fuel the darkness in me, to take my anger out on the world; it was a way of me hurting people to make myself feel better. I was not using boxing for the great sport it was, but for all the wrong reasons.

I saw the girl telling me my friend was dead and watched the internal me crumble as I crawled into a shell filled with darkness and emptiness. I was at the lowest point in my life. Then a beam of light shone on me lying on the torn up mattress. After a few seconds, I saw myself stand up slowly, and my body was filled with light again. I glowed from head to toe and felt negative emotions released from my body that left me feeling light, as if I floated on air.

After, I walked out of the room, out of the front door where I was assaulted by a bright light beaming down on me. I lowered my head to avoid the glare and heard cheering and people shouting my name.

I stopped in my tracks. I was stood on a platform in front of thousands of people. A huge screen hung above; next to it showed a picture of me with the caption, 'Kostas Petrou, Number 1 Motivational Speaker.'

What is happening? Why are these people here? From within me I heard these people are here to listen to you. These people are here because your experiences and words have the ability to touch their lives and help them, and above all, these people are here because you can help them climb their own mountain. This is your calling and we as people shine the brightest when we are fulfilling our life's purpose.

Then I heard my voice; the words were unclear, but I was giving a speech. After I wrapped it up, the crowd went crazy and my body shot up from the mattress.

'What the... what the flipping heck just happened to me?' Did I fall asleep? Did I just experience an epiphany? My head was all over the place, yet I didn't want the moment to end. Standing on the stage talking filled me with a sense of acceptance I'd never experienced before.

I rested my head in my hands, again hoping to relive it - nothing. I stayed still -nothing. I stood up and braced against the wall, nothing. Instead, my head and body ached, reminding me that I'd almost lost my life a second time only a few hours before.

I was dumbfounded by the events, so dumbfounded, that I didn't have any idea how I was actually feeling.

A few minutes later, an incredible surge of something flowed through my body making me feel a level of lightness around my chest, almost as if a bag of bricks had been lifted off of my back and I could stand tall again. But I was aware that this could be shock, as opposed to some mystical sense of freedom.

Chapter 19

CHANGES THAT HEAL

'Small things start us in new ways of thinking'
              — V.S. Naipaul, A Bend in the River

THE VISION PERVADED my thoughts over the coming days, and I couldn't figure out its meaning. Eventually, it faded as time passed.

During a stroll, I was in an upbeat mood, not like what I usually refer to as a walk of shame. Half an hour in, I noticed a man pressure washing a driveway and approached him, 'Excuse me, sorry to bother you, that driveway looks great.'

'Cheers mate.'

'Do you mind my asking how much you can expect to make doing a job like this?'

'Put it this way, I am charging £800 for this drive and it will take me two days.

I gulped. 'What kind of equipment do you need?'

'A pressure washer, water supply, hose pipe, kiln dried sand and, above all, a good work ethic—that's all.'

I thought of my dad's friend who worked at a tool and equipment store. I could probably borrow a pressure washer from him. Excitement flowed through me and I asked, 'What's kiln dried sand?'

'Its sand that goes between the gaps in the block paving after its pressure washed.' He pulled a bag over to show me.

'Thanks mate.' I headed straight to tool shop. To my delight, my dad's friend was on duty.

'Mark, how you doing, mate? I haven't seen you in ages,' I greeted him.

'Kostas, how are you? How is the family?'

'Everybody is great. Strange enough, my dad was saying he has no time to see anybody anymore, including you.'

'Tell me about it, I don't get a chance to do anything nowadays, it's all work and no play,' he replied.

'I must admit though, my dad always speaks highly of you, he said he'll swing by one day to say hello.'

I was stroking his ego to increase my chances of him lending me the pressure washer. He smiled, clearly pleased with the thought of my dad speaking highly of him. I dived straight into the reason for my visit. 'Mark, I am trying to get a business going, but I'm really struggling for cash at the moment. I don't want to ask my dad, he hasn't had the best time lately, you know with the economy and all. Do you reckon you could borrow me a pressure washer? I already have a couple of jobs lined up and as soon as I get paid you have my word I will pay you whatever the cost is for borrowing it.'

'If I get caught mate, I will get into trouble, is there no way of borrowing some money off someone else?'

'If I could Mark, I would. I hate having to ask you, but I have no other option,' I said.

He paused then said, 'Okay Kostas, I will help you, but don't let me down because I will get into a lot of trouble,' he repeated.

'Mate, you don't understand how much I appreciate it.

Thank you so much, I will pick the machine up a day before I need it. Thanks again.' I shook his hand and left. I was beyond happy. I had the resources, now I needed to make it happen.

I walked straight to my granddads house. After catching up with him, I asked him for £2.00. He gave it to me and I hugged him. On the way out, I picked up his yellow pages which he never used and walked to the phone box. I opened the directory and randomly browsed through. My eyes landed on T.G.I Fridays. I put £1.00 in the phone.

'Good Afternoon, T.G.I Friday's, how can I help you?'

'Good afternoon, could I speak to the manager, please?' I asked.

'Can I ask who is calling?'

'Yes, of course, Kostas speaking.' She paused as if waiting for me to say something more. I didn't.

'Okay, hold a moment please.'

'Sure.' I waited for what felt like an eternity as I watched the clock ticking on the phone box.

'Hello, this is John, how can I help you?' a gentleman finally said.

'Hi, my name is Kostas. I run a pressure washing business in the Birmingham area and I noticed that you have a fantastic exterior which could really be a stand out feature of the business. My job is to make that exterior and paving look close to what it looked like when it was new. I'm currently working at Frankie & Benny's doing a similar job. I was wondering if you would be interested in me coming down to discuss the service I provide in more detail,' I blurted out. I had no clue how to sell.

'Sorry, what is the name of your business?' he asked.

My heart sank. I did not consider a company name. 'Would you repeat the question please,' I asked him, to buy a few extra seconds of thinking time.

'What is the name of your company?'

I spotted a van parked outside a café with the words 'Silver Service' emblazoned on the side. 'Silver Surface Cleansing,' I told him quickly.

'Excellent! Okay, come down tomorrow at 10 a.m. and we can come to some agreement.'

I hung up, excited. I flicked through the yellow pages again, found Frankie & Benny's number and ran the exact same pitch to the manager, though I added that I'm currently working with John at T.G.I Fridays. He also agreed to see me.

Within one week, I went from having not a penny to my name to turning £2.00 into two thousand pounds. It was hard work and I had to learn on the job, but I made sure that both jobs were done as perfect as could be. Both managers were extremely happy.

Back in my room, I sat with the money stuffed up my jumper. Words could not explain how great it felt to actually create a job myself and be in a position where I could build and grow.

I pondered on what to spend the money on. Should I splash out on fresh, new clothes and a nice new bed? Never jump in for the easiest and fastest route, find the route that will teach you.

Hmm… if I made the room comfortable I wouldn't have a big enough need to change. I became mindful that I was thinking along the lines of going the large route. After some thinking, I made a conscious decision to invest in my self-development.

I walked into Waterstones in the city centre and bought ten books in one go that included, English, mathematics, sales, success in life and successful people, including Dale Carnegie's book 'How to win friends and influence people.'

I got more jobs and made good money, though it was inconsistent. When I wasn't working, I studied and read for hours and practiced what I learnt when out and about. Soon my world began to change. Things seemed brighter for the first time in a long while. I took pride in myself again and deeply believed I could be successful. I felt as if a seed of wisdom was planted within me and with each day that seed sprouted. I had moments when I felt like throwing the towel in, but I came up with the mantra, 'Don't just go through it, grow through it!' to keep me going. I started to behave as if I was a successful person, or more of a high flyer.

As I sat in Costa Coffee shop reading 'Think and Grow Rich' one day, I overheard a guy at a table behind me tell his friend, 'You need to get into recruitment, mate. I am on a 6-figure salary as a consultant.'

I smelt opportunity and soon after walked into a recruitment agency not far from the coffee shop. I asked an employee what was the best route into recruitment. She told me that I would have to start as a trainee and work my way up. The salary wasn't anything to get excited about, but I looked at the bigger picture.

From there, I took a trip to the library where I researched what recruiting entailed. It seemed like a cool occupation, helping people to find work and selling at the same time. I like helping people. Thereafter, I researched jobs in the Birmingham area for recruitment consultants on the Internet. I found one requesting applicants to send in their C.Vs. I didn't have one.

Undeterred, I called the manager. 'Hi, Matt, my name is Kostas. I noticed you are currently recruiting for a consultant and I'd like to find out more information about the role.'

'I'm afraid that position is about to be filled. I've already found somebody.'

About to be filled! 'Okay, but if you don't mind my asking, what is the salary for the role?'

He told me and I said, 'I believe I would be excellent at it. I'll take 3K less and not a penny of commission for the first 6-months. I built a business from the ground up. The problem is it's seasonal.'

'Hmm, okay, Kostas, can you come and meet me in a couple of days and bring a C.V with you?'

'Sure. No problem at all.'

I met Matt and he offered me the job. I felt as if I was reprieved. I proved to myself and my family that I could stand on my own feet. I could finally move on from the abandoned building.

Chapter 20

PATHFINDER

'There's nothing better when something comes and hits you and you think 'YES'!'

— *J.K. Rowling*

I WAS BROKEN but now I was in a position to rebuild my life, ready to take on the world.

As it happened, Granddad was not very well and was going through a tough time health-wise. I decided to move in with him. While I worked during the day, the day carers looked after him. With me being there, he had twenty-four-hour supervision and attention.

I threw myself into my new role as recruitment consultant and worked hard. Within six months, I was in charge of the biggest contract the company had. I was on the up and up.

One morning, I woke up and could barely breathe. My body was aching and my temperature was sky high. When I stood up, I felt as if I was going to pass out. I went straight to the doctors.

'Kostas, I am going to have to call an ambulance for you, you have pneumonia,' the doctor told me after a few tests.

'No way, I am not getting in any ambulance and I do not need to go to the hospital. Give me some antibiotics. I'll be fine,' I said to her. I did not want to go. Every time I went to hospitals I ended up more sick. Even if I visited someone I became ill.

'Kostas you don't understand, within days you could be critical if the antibiotics don't work.'

'Doctor, I understand completely, but I assure you that if you give me antibiotics I will be fine.'

'Okay, but if you do not start to feel better in 3-days then you have to go in,' she told me in a serious voice.

I nodded. I was ill for two weeks and concerned about my job. It was a cut throat environment and no one cared whether you were sick or not. If you were not making money, you were shipped out.

As soon as I entered the office on my first day back, the manager called me into his office. 'Kostas, you have done a fantastic job for us, but the lady who was on maternity leave is returning. She has been with us for 7-years. As much as I would like to keep you on, I have to let her return to her post, which unfortunately you are covering.'

I was disheartened, but I learnt so much during the time I was there I felt confident enough to move on. I thanked him for giving me the opportunity and the experience and went back to the drawing board.

Three weeks later, I landed an admin position. It wasn't my ideal job, but the job market was shaky and I was grateful to be employed and financially independent. Life was good.

While relaxing and chatting to friends on Facebook one day, a picture of an amazingly stunning girl appeared. Really, she was shockingly beautiful. I sent her a message. She replied, and before long we were in full conversation, which went on for weeks. Eventually, I asked for her number and we hit it off, often talking into the early morning hours. I never believed I could meet someone who could make every day feel so special.

I still struggled to make eye contact with people, but I desperately wanted to meet Elisavet, Elizabeth in English. We met at a posh bar, The Cube. After a couple of drinks, we went on to Estilo's for a meal. I could not look at her properly. I did not feel worthy to be with her. She was like an angel and I did not deserve an angel in my life, or at least I felt I didn't. 'I think you are really beautiful and to be honest I have never told anybody that before,' I said to her.

She smiled, and I felt as if I could tell her my life story and she would not judge me. She looked at me with a glow in her eyes and something inside told me that this was the beginning of something special.

Six months later, we got engaged. It was the happiest day of my life because I knew that with her beside me I could achieve anything. She helped me to further believe in myself.

A couple of months later, I moved in with her and her family in a beautiful house. One starlit night, while driving, I reflected on how my life had taken a 360-degree turn, from being homeless to having a fiancée, to living in an amazing house in a beautiful area. It was a dream come true.

Not long after, I landed my next job in recruitment. When the manager agreed to hire me, he said, 'Kostas, we will give you a chance.' This fueled a certain emotion within me, as I'd be working with people who were far more educated than myself, many of whom held degrees.

Undaunted, I made a decision to outwork every single person in that building. I got to work at 7a.m. and left at 8p.m. When I encountered challenges, I recited a mantra to motivate me: You may out skill me, but you will never out will me!

After one year, the annual report came through on the year's performance. 'I would first off like to congratulate Kostas, who is a huge success story for this company. He came in as a wild card and after year one, I am pleased to say that he is the highest performer this company has ever had.

'He has driven this company to have the best year it has ever had and this is a result of unbelievable hard work. I want this to be an example to you all that if you want to be successful and you are willing to put in the sacrifice and hard work, you can achieve anything you want. He is living proof of that!' the manager announced.

I was gob smacked! I could not believe it. I was the highest performer ever. Not long after, I was getting headhunted from various companies and I even got an offer from one of the 'Dragons Den's' star of the British television series, to go into business. I was flying high. I was chuffed with my achievement.

One day, while speaking to a candidate, she confessed that she lacked confidence and it affected her during interviews. I helped her with some words of wisdom and after she said, 'You should be a motivational speaker. I would pay to see you.'

I enjoyed coaching her, though I didn't view it as such at the time. The comment she made stuck with me and I began to research motivational speaking. While doing so, the vision of me walking onto a platform with thousands of people waiting to hear me speak rose to the forefront of my mind and the overall mirage finally made sense - it was a parable of my life. The dark cloud, the mountain, the first figure, the fall, the climb... and the second figure represented my father! It was he who spoke those pearls of wisdom.

All along, Dad was encouraging me to become the person he knew I was capable of becoming. He did the best thing any father could do for his son - allowed me to discover the world through my own eyes, no matter how hard it was for him.

I felt so ashamed. For so long, I blamed the one person who actually saved my life. Instead of blaming him for my struggles, I needed to thank him for giving me the characteristics necessary to overcome them.

This realization exploded into a supernova of understanding and it became crystal clear to me that my life's purpose is to motivate others, to help them achieve their goals. An overwhelming and bitter sweet feeling overcame me – I finally found my true path.

Cherry-Ann Carew collaborated with Kostas Petrou on Rise From The Dream. She is an award finalist, multi-bestselling author and Founder of Writetastic Solutions, a company that helps authors build their book business by creating multiple income streams.

She is also co-author of the Amazon best-selling book How The fierce Handle Fear: Secrets to Succeeding in Challenging Times, that includes, Donald Trump, business magnate, and Jack Canfield, co-creator of the Chicken Soup for the Soul book series.

Cherry-Ann lives in California. Visit her website at: http://www.writetasticsolutions.com

Printed in Great Britain
by Amazon.co.uk, Ltd.,
Marston Gate.